Praise fo

Walker Hayes is captivating. I k.......... ....came on the Today Show. But that brilliance on the screen was only a tiny fraction of who he really is. The real stuff is on the pages of this book. Both Walker and Craig are lit from inside . . . that light is splashed on each and every page. You will feel it and be inspired!

HODA KOTB
Coanchor, NBC News' *Today*; cohost, *Today with Hoda & Jenna*

An incredible story of friendship, faith, the love of Jesus and the sovereign hand of God, *Glad You're Here* is a book that will bring tears to your eyes and breath to your lungs and make you see and love your neighbors just a little different—and maybe a lot better.

ANNIE F. DOWNS
New York Times bestselling author of *That Sounds Fun*

The first time I heard the song "Craig" was a few years before I had the privilege of meeting Walker. The song stopped me in my tracks. I'd never heard a song capture how the church is supposed to be, and it came from a man who didn't know Jesus at the time. Well, Walker does know Jesus now, thanks to the Lord using his friend Craig, and has an incredible story to tell.

BART MILLARD
Lead singer of MercyMe

Glad You're Here comes as a gift to a world that seems quicker to divide than come together. Walker and Craig weren't obvious candidates for close friend-ship: an avowed atheist and a committed believer, a musician struggling to find his place and a pastor who questioned his calling, both bringing past hurts and vulnerabilities into their present relationships. But theirs is a story of genuine affection, sacrificial love, sacred hospitality, and a celebration of the God-given gift of one another. Whether you follow Jesus or regard Him with skepticism, the impact He has on these men is undeniable—and their story might just inspire you to learn more about the One who turned water Napa Valley red.

PETER GREER
President & CEO of HOPE International and coauthor of *Mission Drift*

Meet Walker (country singer-songwriter) and Craig. They tell a story of how the gospel transforms people through the gift of friendship. Their writing is clear, transparent, and engaging, inspiring hope for what can happen as God makes us better witnesses in a broken world. This is a captivating book that will be of help to anyone wise enough to pick it up!

DAVE HARVEY
President of Great Commission Collective; author of *The Plurality Principle* and *I Still Do*

One of the greatest gifts God has given to you and me is the gift of friendship. Walker and Craig invite all of us into the depths of what Christ-centered friendship is all about in this powerful book. I found myself crying on one page and hysterically laughing on the next! My only complaint is the book had to end!

BRIAN CLARKE
Pastor, Cross Point Church

In *Glad You're Here*, Craig and Walker refuse to be trite. They tell their stories honestly, giving us full view of the joys and the heartaches accompanying the surprising friendship of a pastor and a country music star. Their account will leave you heartened and challenged to pursue the authentic faith and unvarnished friendship they've discovered together. This book is a delight to read!

CHRIS HORST
Coauthor of *Rooting for Rivals*

I love this book so much. The honesty, the rawness, the storyline—it's written vulnerably and beautifully, and it all just points to the goodness of Jesus!

STEVE FEE
Songwriter / Producer, Nashville, TN

GLAD YOU'RE

TWO UNLIKELY FRIENDS BREAKING BREAD AND FENCES

Walker Hayes & Craig Allen Cooper

MOODY PUBLISHERS
CHICAGO

Unless otherwise indicated, Scripture quotations are from the ESV® Bible (The Holy Bible, English Standard Version®), copyright © 2001 by Crossway, a publishing minis-try of Good News Publishers. Used by permission. All rights reserved.
All emphasis in Scripture has been added.

Names and details of some stories have been changed to protect the privacy of indi-viduals.

Edited by Mackenzie Conway
Interior design: Puckett Smartt
Cover design: Erik M. Peterson
Author photo for Walker Hayes: Robert Chavers
Author photo for Craig Cooper: Laura Cooper, McKain Photography

All websites and phone numbers listed herein are accurate at the time of publication but may change in the future or cease to exist. The listing of website references and resources does not imply publisher endorsement of the site's entire contents. Groups and organizations are listed for informational purposes, and listing does not imply publisher endorsement of their activities.

ISBN: 978-0-8024-2471-6

Originally delivered by fleets of horse-drawn wagons, the affordable paperbacks from D. L. Moody's publishing house resourced the church and served everyday people. Now, after more than 125 years of publishing and ministry, Moody Publishers' mission remains the same—even if our delivery systems have changed a bit. For more infor-mation on other books (and resources) created from a biblical perspective, go to www .moodypublishers.com or write to:

Moody Publishers
820 N. LaSalle Boulevard
Chicago, IL 60610

3 5 7 9 10 8 6 4

Printed in the United States of America

Dedicated to the One who walked on water
and turned it Napa Valley red.

CONTENTS

1

_A_
DREAM

WALKER

It was a Friday night way down south in Mobile, Alabama. I was shyly sitting in the corner of the Mobile Yacht Club off of Dauphin Island Parkway. Through a dirty window, I could see headlights crossing the causeway bridge against an almost black sky. I had my Taylor acoustic guitar and a Shure SM58 mic plugged into a tiny crate amplifier to the left of my bar stool. Directly in front of me was a black metal music stand that held the printed-out lyrics to "The Dock of the Bay" by Otis Redding and Steve Cropper. The place was so empty it looked closed. There were six people in the entire seating area and maybe one or two at the bar. When I finished playing the song, Trudy, the bartender and manager, noticed no one was clapping. She tucked her tray under her arm and applauded with an "I feel sorry for you" smile. A few random, slow golf claps trickled in behind hers as they noticed I was finished.

I couldn't even consider myself mediocre. My nervous fingers messed up every chord that night. My voice was what it is, nothing special. My banter was incredibly awkward, and my tip jar was empty, but I was hooked. The adrenaline was like nothing I'd ever experienced.

Before I even loaded my gear into my trunk that night, I called my fiancée, Laney, from the parking lot and said, "I want to be a singer." I paused. "Wanna move to Nashville?"

Without hesitation, Laney said, "Absolutely."

I think the craziest thing about the night my dream was conceived is that I really didn't even want to play the show in the first place. It was born out of one of those classic "dad bragging about his kid" moments. He was at the yacht club one night and just decided that he thought I was as good as anyone he'd ever heard singing and playing there, so he booked me a gig without even asking if I wanted one. To say I was mad at him for doing this would be a ginormous understatement. I couldn't believe he'd signed me up for that. First of all, I was a grown man. I didn't need my "daddy" to be my booking agent. Second of all, I had serious stage fright. I'm talking terrified, fingers shaking, forgetting all the words, stage fright. Third of all, I was not that talented. I was "my mom, my dad, and my girlfriend think I'm good" good, but that's it.

Nothing about me indicated that I should aim for the stars. However, my dad thought I should, so he nudged me; and I'm glad he did. I told him I would only play the show on one condition: that he had to stop bugging me to play live. I played the show, but he never stopped bugging me.

As I recall talking to Laney on the phone that night, all I can wonder is, "What in the world were we thinking?" I was twenty-three years old, off to a promising start selling real estate with my dad, and newly engaged to my high school sweetheart. We had even put a down payment on a lot we'd found about a half a mile around the corner from my office and were narrowing down house plans. My new dream and the timing of it made zero sense whatsoever. It blindsided me and everyone else. I remember telling our change of plans to family and friends and them not being able to hide the shock on their faces. Some people literally laughed out loud because they thought I was joking. I specifically remember the question, "Do you even sing in front of people?" I said, "No, not really, but I will." My mother was happy for us in a worried way. I remember her concerned smiles.

Laney's parents were completely sucker-punched. They were still trying to wrap their brains around their daughter's questionable taste in boys. I had just assured them a month or two earlier, when I asked for Laney's hand, that we were going to live in Mobile, I would be selling real estate with my dad, and their future grandbabies would be growing up right around the corner. So, you can imagine their reaction when their soon-to-be son-in-law drops by mid-week and casually informs them that he thinks he wants to move to Nashville and become a rockstar. Nope, it wasn't the most comfortable dinner I've had with them, but I am confident they handled it better than I would have in their situation. I wish I could remember exactly how I attempted to smoothly transition the conversation from casual small talk to, "So, I have this illusive dream I'd like to run by y'all . . ."

As a father of daughters, I feel bad for putting them in that situation. It's pretty laughable looking back. What did I expect them to say? "Oh, that's a wonderful idea! What realistic ambitions you have! According to statistics, that sounds like a lovely future for our baby girl!" Their response wasn't entirely supportive, but it was way more merciful than I imagine I would have been. Let me put it this way: If I saw the seventeen-year-old version of me standing at the door to pick up my oldest daughter, Lela (sixteen), I'd shut it in his face and tell Lela it was just a Girl Scout selling cookies. Or, who knows, maybe I'd feel compassion knowing too well how scary it was to walk up those steps. Maybe I'd just hope he loves her as much as I love Laney.

Emotionally, I think Laney and I may have been running away from some things. Me especially. I'm no psychologist, so I truly have no idea how to properly diagnose what I was dealing with mentally at the time;

but a clean slate and mattering in the world sounded inviting to me. As a kid, I truly believed I would make it to the NBA, and that ended abruptly. Mobile, Alabama, knew me too well as the rebellious youngster I was; and Laney and I weren't really the ideal picture of forever when it came to our dating relationship.

We were on- and off-again a lot, either making up or breaking up. So much so that we were embarrassed to update our family and friends on our status. We were extremely volatile and our engagement came as a complete surprise to many. We were even a little bit tentative when telling others we were engaged because we dreaded the doubtful looks on their faces. A lot of people were most definitely thinking, "Hmm, I wonder how long this is going to last." We couldn't blame them. Then, to add to our stack of impressive life decisions, we thought I was going to be the next Kenny Chesney.

Getting away sounded like a fresh start and felt like freedom from the dream crushers. Becoming famous was the opposite of what most people would have predicted I'd become. Well, famous in a good way. I think a lot of artists can relate to this emotion. The "I'm going to show them" drive. This dream and our brokenness created the perfect storm. Laney and I hesitated less about moving to Nashville than we did about picking out a wedding cake. I really don't remember ever asking ourselves if we were crazy or really caring if people thought we were. We were excited, naive, and loving all the firsts. (I remember getting giddy in Wal-Mart buying our first toiletries together. I had no idea how many different soaps, luffas, and shampoos a woman needs. I still don't really know what conditioner is.)

This dream and our brokenness created the perfect storm.

So, we drove our U-Haul, straight from our honeymoon, full of toiletries and hand-me-down furniture, to our one-room apartment in downtown Nashville. We were the cheesiest, brightest-eyed, bush-iest-tailed newlyweds you ever saw. Nothing could bring us down. We applied for jobs, crashed every open mic night in town, and began making connections. Within weeks, I discovered an obsessive passion for song-writing at The Bluebird Cafe. That historic venue changed my life. It was there that I first heard some of Nashville's most prolific songwriters performing massive hits they had written. I literally walked out of that place writing my first song on a napkin, and I haven't stopped since. We were going to make it. We just knew it. I wrote songs and sang them to Laney while she made chocolate chip pound cake in apartment 9. Ignorance was bliss.

Nashville. More like, "threw me in trash-ville." Fast forward ten years, a hundred heartbreaks, and five kids later. Reality had hunted us down. I couldn't get arrested. As a singer, I had been dropped by Mercury Records and Capitol Records and had been passed on at least twice by every other record label in town. As a songwriter, I had written hundreds and hundreds of songs for multiple publishing companies, but none of them made it to the radio. I'd burned bridges with two managers, wrongfully blaming them for my failures, and had run out of promising contacts. I couldn't sleep, struggling with the question, "What is best for my kids? Do I teach them to never give up, no matter what, or do I teach them there is actually a time to give up?" We proved every single person who sarcastically said "good luck" that they were right. Money was tight and so was hope.

When my dream was new, I loved it. I protected it. I appreciated how it set me apart. Even the thought of it thrilled me, no matter how far away it seemed. I thrived on every second of the chase. Even hearing "no" fueled me to work harder. But eventually, I hated my dream. I didn't want it anymore. I remember desperately wishing I could fall out of love with music, wishing it would leave me alone, wishing I could stop writing lyrics on every piece of trash in my car, only to find myself writing a song about those emotions on the side of a styrofoam cup.

I thought about going home to Mobile, but I was too proud. I would rather have lived with my family under a bridge than return to Mobile defeated. I thought about getting a desk job, but I couldn't afford the amount of Adderall I would have needed for that (I've been prescribed Adderall in the past). I didn't know what to do. My dream had made a fool out of me. I wanted to punch it in the face.

CRAIG

WHEN OUR FAMILY made the decision to move to Nashville in 2012, like Walker, I too was chasing a dream. It was late autumn and the leaves had turned their golden hue. A cool breeze circulated in the midday air, and the sensation within our hearts was electric. My wife, Laura, and I had just finished loading all of our belongings in the back of a U-Haul truck. We buckled our four kids safely in the family van and paused to stare at the home we were within seconds of leaving behind. As I often do, I captured the moment with a quick pic on my phone. We thanked God for all the good we had experienced over the course of our seventeen years of living in east Tennessee, and we prayed for blessings on our move. It's difficult to describe the mixture of emotions we were experiencing, though Laura and I tried hard to put them into words along the drive. She steered the van, and I drove the U-Haul, so we had plenty of time to process everything over the phone as we made the trek across the state of Tennessee to the rental house we would now call home. When I wasn't talking with Laura, I was listening to Fleetwood Mac's song "Landslide" on repeat, absorbing it as an anthem for boldly embracing this changing season of my life.

I'm a feeler by nature, so I felt it all very deeply. Everything I had known in my adult life was fading quickly in the rearview mirror of a rented U-Haul. There was a strange mixture of apprehension and exhilaration, of sadness and joy, of loss and gain, of concern and relief all experienced concurrently, kind of like the sensation you get when you taste Sour Patch Kids for the first time. Whenever you bite into something like that, you're not really sure what's hitting your taste buds at first; once it all settles down, you can then decide whether you like it or not. I happen to love Sour Patch Kids, and it wasn't long before our family decided we really liked the flavor of Nashville as well.

My dream was to help start a church to share the good news of God's immeasurable love in Jesus—to see lives transformed by that love. When we moved to Nashville, I wasn't dreaming of city lights. I wasn't dreaming of celebrity sightings or world-class concerts under the stars. I wasn't dreaming of social media influence or global impact. (I admit that at the time I didn't even realize how significant of a city Nashville is in those regards). I'm a very simple man. I spent my childhood in a small town called Ooltewah before attending college in Knoxville. I didn't have a category at all for interacting with people of widespread influence. Once our family settled into the Nashville area, I was so clueless about my surroundings that whenever I saw someone familiar, I assumed we had met before. Like the time I was putting cream in my coffee at Starbucks in downtown Franklin and I recognized the lady next to me as she was waiting for her turn with the dispenser.

"I know I know you, but I can't remember how we've met . . . are you from Knoxville, by chance?" I asked. When she kindly informed me that she was *not* from Knoxville, I kept persisting with my inquiry about where in the world we could have met.

Finally, she graciously replied, "Well, I am an actress; maybe that's how you recognize me?"

Honestly, I was a bit stunned and didn't know what to say. One of my new friends overhearing the conversation stepped in and listed off several shows and movies she had acted in, and that's how I met Kimberly Williams-Paisley (the wife of country singer Brad Paisley and the actress who, among many roles, famously played Annie in the movie *Father of the Bride*, which happens to be one of my wife's favorite movies).

"Toto, I've a feeling we're not in Kansas anymore."

* * *

My dream was sparked during my freshman year of college in 1995. Through a series of events, I began to see that I was lost spiritually— as lost in my eighteen-year-old soul as I was lost as an eight-year-old when separated from my family on the beach. (This really did happen. I searched helplessly through a sea of people on Myrtle Beach for hours before my family finally found me.)

I grew up in the South in a region often referred to as the "Bible Belt." Churches were located on nearly every corner, and our family attended church regularly. By all accounts, I would have been considered a decent kid. I graduated at the top of my class in high school, a valedictorian, senior class vice president, and a leader in our youth group at church, but it was all more out of the personal pursuit of moralism and social acceptance than a genuine relationship with God. Outwardly, I checked off a lot of "good guy" boxes, but inwardly I was just walking further and further away from God. By the time I stepped foot on a college campus, I was miserably lost. I was familiar with Jesus, but I related to Him like someone does a distant relative (happy to claim a connection but with no recent visitations and no real-time relationship). You could say I was a nominal Christian (a Christian "in name only"). I didn't have a problem with Jesus; I just didn't know Him.

One day as I was interacting with an elderly woman at work, she asked me a searching question:

"That cross around your neck"—pausing and pointing to the wooden necklace I wore from a rope chain—"is that decoration, or is it *real*?"

"A little bit of both?" I answered hesitantly, wondering if that was even an option in her mind . . . or God's.

She left not long after our brief interaction, but the question lingered in my mind. I could not get it out of my head:

"That cross around your neck . . . is it decoration, or is it real?"

It wasn't long after this conversation that I was invited to attend an event hosted by a campus ministry, and it was there that God drew near to me in the most loving of ways. As I heard preaching from the Gospel of John, I saw myself in a man named Nicodemus. John tells us that Nicodemus was a member of the religious ruling council. He was an upstanding man, well respected in the community, yet as Jesus spoke with him about eternal life, Nicodemus couldn't even make sense of what Jesus was talking about. Jesus asked him a probing question: "Are you the teacher of Israel and yet you do not understand these things?" Then Jesus went right to the heart of the matter to show Nicodemus his spiritual need. He said that unless Nicodemus was born again (given the gift of eternal life from God above), he wouldn't be able to see or enter the kingdom of God (John 3:1–21).

> "That cross around your neck . . . is that decoration, or is it real?"

That night I began to realize that just because you know *of* Jesus does not mean you truly *know* Jesus (Matt. 7:21–23). I saw my need for Jesus, not just as my example (which is how I saw Him before), but as my Savior. I understood for the first time that I could go to church every Sunday morning, Sunday night, and Wednesday night, and still not be a Christian—not have a true relationship with God through Jesus. Though I wore a cross around my neck daily at the time, it had only been for decoration. That night, I grasped the true meaning of the cross like I never had before. I understood that Jesus had died on the cross to pay the penalty I owed for all the ways I had dishonored and strayed from God, even in the pursuit of my own "goodness." Jesus captured my full attention and ravished my soul with so much joy that I surrendered my entire life to Him that evening. The cross was no longer a decoration around my neck. It was a declaration of God's great love for me in sending His Son to pay the price for my salvation, and I became a genuine follower of Jesus.

When someone asked me that evening, "What's God doing in your heart?" I answered, "I just want to give my life to Jesus, and I want to do what that man just did" (pointing to the preacher who had just shared the gospel with me). I knew I wanted to tell others of the good news that Jesus is real, that He hears and answers our prayers, that His love can transform our lives, that He came to seek and save the lost, and that true life can be found in Him.

I had discovered my dream, and that's the dream I was carrying with me when our family moved to Nashville to help start a church called Redeeming Grace.

CHURCH

WALKER

My oldest son, Chapel (six at the time), played in an upward basketball league in Brentwood, Tennessee. Our family was quite a herd. It was always tough to keep all the kids off the court while teams were practicing or playing. I remember loving when practices would end, having the court to ourselves till someone would kindly kick us out by retrieving all the basketballs. I would usually meet Laney and the kids at practice after a day of writing songs and drinking. My job at basketball practices and games was holding our four-month-old little girl, Loxley (aka Lolly), while she slept. I'll never forget those moments. The smell of newborn baby mixed with the wood floor. I always stood in the same corner of the gym rocking Lolly in my dad's hand-me-down blue jean jacket. I often wondered how many times my dad had held me as a baby while wearing it.

I loved my role at the gym for three reasons. One, holding Loxley always distracted me from my failures. Gently shifting my weight side to side with her in my arms lowered my blood pressure. Two, making sure Lolly didn't wake up kept me from yelling at Chapel from the sidelines, so living vicariously through him was contained to an occasional, quiet, disapproving head shake. Three, people were less likely to want to make small talk since I was clearly holding a sleeping baby. A nod or a whispered, "Hey, good to see ya" with a smile got the job done.

I avoided small talk like COVID. I didn't love chatting it up with random people because, nine times out of ten, once a new acquaintance found out I was a singer/songwriter, they'd always follow up with, "Oh, have you written anything I've heard?"

Answering "nope" to this question over and over through the years had taken its toll. When you tell someone you're a singer/songwriter, their eyes light up at the thought that they might be in the presence of a celebrity. Then, when you have to inform them that you're not famous, they deflate like a whoopie cushion. Sarcastically, I would think to myself, "So sorry to have let you down; wish I could have mattered more for you." I was beyond sick and tired of the "So, what do you do?" conversation, so I hid happily under my shaggy hair in my corner of the gym with Loxley.

Laney, on the other hand, is completely the opposite. She could chat with a brick wall.

I sometimes can't believe the conversations I would overhear her having on the bleachers with complete strangers or new-ish friends. Maybe it's a mom thing, but I am blown away with how she and a brand-new friend can go from, "Hey, my name is so-and-so," immediately to "My last delivery was vaginal," while neither of them bat an eye at the word "vaginal." I feel weird just typing that word. Laney would be talking to someone from the minute she walked into the gym to the second she shut her car door to leave. I would eavesdrop every now and then for entertainment purposes but would rarely engage. I'd generally found that the relationships Laney made at these events were here and gone with the basketball season. She and a few women would share the bleachers for a couple months or so and then go their separate ways. However, that wasn't the case with Laura Cooper.

Laney saw Laura at one of Chapel's basketball games. I can't recall the exact date but I am certain it was a Saturday morning in late January 2014. Laura's son, Joshua, played basketball in the same upward league, and Laura recognized Laney from having met her briefly through a mutual friend. I don't remember meeting Laura. I would guess I was hiding from social interaction in the corner with Lolly. On the way home from the game, Laney told me about Laura and that she had invited us to a new church that evening.

Church . . .

I hated the word. I hated how it made me feel. The word triggered guilt, shame, anger, and hurt. It reminded me of living in constant trouble as a child. It brought back the sting of dad's belt when I couldn't sit still enough. It reminded me of a youth pastor and pediatrician I had looked up to until I saw his profile in the local newspaper as a convicted pedophile. It brought back the faces of "godly" friends who tried to move in on Laney the minute she and I broke up. It walked me back through the tons of churches we had visited in the Nashville area that sounded and felt more like American Idol auditions. "Church" stood for the transformation I could never attain as a defiant teenager, the hypocrisy I'd since met inside it, and a god, who, I was sure, could not exist. To say the least, like many people, I suffered from church PTSD.

So, as you can imagine, I wasn't a huge fan of this Laura Cooper lady. At this point in our marriage, our only massive disagreements were about drinking and Jesus. Sounds like a song title: "Drinking and Jesus." We didn't fight about money because we didn't have any. I was pretty irritated when Laney mentioned she'd like to visit Redeeming Grace. They met on Saturday nights, which meant I only had a few hours to argue my way out.

> *At this point in our marriage, our only massive disagreements were about drinking and Jesus.*

I fought it hard, tried to convince Laney it was all a crock, and even tried to persuade her to relax and just kick it at home instead, but nothing worked. There were churches we'd attended in phases per Laney's wishes, but we had never gotten past the "visitors" stage. After a while, she had become content with the fact that we would never find a place where we truly connected, and I was thrilled with her complacency. To put it mildly, I was really bummed when Laura pulled us back in the church market. I kind of thought we had finished that "church shopping" phase of life. I really just wished the "church monster" would leave our relationship alone. Like I said, drinking and Jesus, that's all we fought about. Otherwise, we were cool.

I kicked and screamed the entire way to Redeeming Grace. Laney drove us there because I'd been drinking all afternoon. It felt like we drove forever, because we literally drove forever. The building they met in was in the middle of nowhere, and in the early darkness of winter, the outside of it resembled a church you might find in a 1970s horror movie. The lengthy trip and the spooky vibes only supported my argument for declining Laura's invitation. Even Laney was a little bit hesitant as we parked in the lot. I remember she even stopped being mad at me long enough to laugh with me and agree when I suggested, "We might wanna call someone and at least tell them where we are before we go missing." Even our big kids in the back were like, "Um, y'all sure this is the right place?"

We were late for the service. That's just how we rolled. Just another reason I wasn't a fan of visiting churches. When you have five kids (eight and under), you're always late, and when you're late, no matter what door you walk in, it's always a grand entrance. Lots of head turning and awkward stares. My personal favorite is watching people count our kids in disbelief. With our family, there is no such thing as slipping in quietly.

We walked in during the praise and worship portion of the service, a particular part of church I loathed and wouldn't have minded missing one bit. It was just a white dude with an acoustic guitar in a golf hat. I didn't want to admit it, but I was actually impressed with how unimpressive it was. Since moving to Nashville, it had really been a long time since I'd stepped in a church that didn't feel like the Dove Awards. It was simple and honest. Speaking as someone who is helpless to the emotional tug of music, I've always thought church music had a way of taking advantage of people like me. The preacher begins to pray, a piano softly enters the background, the acoustic guitar begins to strum, the soundtrack crescendos simultaneously with the preacher's volume, and by the end you're walking down an aisle, wondering what in the world is happening to your heart. For someone like me, the Holy Spirit and music can be confused with one another. Regardless, that night, the music just wasn't about the music, in a refreshing way.

In the middle of praise and worship, the pastor stood up on stage in front of maybe a quarter-full chapel and instructed everyone to stand and greet their neighbor. I thought to myself sarcastically, "Great, they greet each other." I can't say I remember exactly how it went down because I was a little tipsy and that was years ago, but I'm going to go out on a limb and say Craig's hand was the first hand I shook. That's just who he is. Dude would be the greatest Costco greeter of all time. No joke. I dare you to come to Redeeming Grace and try to meet a visitor before he does. You won't do it. I'll give you fifty bucks if you beat him.

But the difference in Craig, the Christ in Craig, that I met that night looked me dead in the eyes knowing I was drunk, knowing I was not a believer, knowing I was as uncomfortable in those creaky old wooden pews as I was in my own skin, knowing I thought his beliefs were as crazy as believing in Santa Claus, and said, "I'm glad you're here." He meant it. And by the grace of God, for the first time in my life, I believed it. Typing that makes me tear up a little bit. I know it might sound meaningless and like a non-event, but at that moment, something inside me began to soften.

I don't remember the sermon. But I do remember meeting the head pastor, Dave. There were pretty similar vibes coming from him as I got with Craig. We hit it off talking Alabama football, and I just got the sense there was no need pretending with these cats. No, my life didn't look like theirs as far as all that believing-in-Jesus part, but I didn't feel "worse" than them in their circle. They didn't look down on me; they just looked at me like they looked at each other. It was fresh.

After the service, I found my boys down a hallway in this large room full of kids in the back of the building playing a sick game of foursquare. There were a few adults back there but none of them told the kids to stop running or to talk with their inside voices. I was like, "Let's do this." I hopped in line and showed no mercy. For the first time in her life, Laney had to beg me to leave church. Usually, it was the other way around.

"Welcomed" was a tough emotion to process. I guess since I was used to, and maybe even quite comfortable with, not feeling welcome, the foreign concept of acceptance was a lot to process. My natural human tendency is to be an island. I don't blame my childhood. I don't blame my parents. I don't blame the church I grew up in or anywhere or anyone that has ever hurt me. I just prefer to keep my distance.

I am hurtful. I can push people away like it's nobody's business. I've never been dropped, fired, dumped, left, beat up, or injured without begging for it. Ask Laney. I am not one of those wounded people in a movie you want to root for. I am a masterful sinner in need of a Savior whose love is unconditionally crazy. This truth only magnifies my gratitude to God for giving Craig and the Redeeming Grace squad the grace to care about a cold, angry, arrogant, disinterested soul like mine. It was just so surprising that it was a little difficult to accept.

I wasn't proud of myself for liking how it felt. And, I wasn't a hundred percent sure I believed I was actually welcome. I was still second-guessing whether I could actually trust them.

Laney, like always, asked me on the way home that night what I thought of the Redeeming Grace experience. I can't remember exactly what my answer was. Knowing myself then, I'm sure I was way too proud to admit that I didn't hate it. But regardless, we returned the next Saturday. I didn't kick and scream, and I wore my foursquare shoes.

CRAIG

LIKE WALKER, I UNDERSTAND FEELINGS of apprehension walking into a church service. On a recent trip, I visited a church for the first time. In the parking lot, I debated whether to bring my coffee in with me. The early morning hours and a strong desire for caffeine won the battle, so I carried my steel tumbler in with one hand, my Bible and notebook in the other. After singing, the congregation was seated and the pastor stood up to address the church. At that exact moment, I reached for my notebook without looking and knocked my coffee mug to the ground with a noticeable thunk. I watched in embarrassment as all my coffee began to spill. It was my first time there, and I had already made a complete mess of my surroundings. Instinctively, I tried to cover the spill with my Bible and notebook so that no one would see it. Then I had the thought, "Yep, whenever I walk into a church, I bring my mess with me."

I know what it's like to feel guilt, shame, and hurt inside the four walls of a church. I'm all too familiar with the look in the eyes of someone thinking, "I don't wanna be here right now." I've seen that look staring back at me in the mirror.

Long before Redeeming Grace was established, I was fired from my first pastoral ministry role. It's been over twenty years since that took place, yet even as I type, I can feel the full force of the pain of it all. After graduation from college, I was on the fast track to public and pastoral ministry. The lead pastor of our growing church encouraged me in these pursuits, providing regular opportunities for me to preach, teach, and lead in various ministry settings. I was willing and eager, a young believer in Jesus full of passion and zeal, and it wasn't long before I was invited to attend a school for the theological and practical training of pastors. It felt like everything was falling into place in my early twenties. I had fallen in love with Laura and had been offered a position as a pastor in the church that I loved. Laura and I got married, and ten days after our honeymoon, I started serving in full-time ministry. I wanted to do great things for Jesus and my aim was to be a pastor for the rest of my life. If you looked up the word *zeal* in the dictionary in those days, I'm quite sure you could have seen a picture of my face beside it.

But six months into my new role, the wheels were starting to shake. I had responsibilities that far exceeded my wisdom, stature, and experience, and I was having a tough time with it all. Nearly every evening of our first and second years of marriage was booked with ministry responsibilities, with the exception of one at the end of the week when Laura and I connected for a date night—exhausted. I was leading worship team practices on Monday nights, conducting a Bible study in a college dorm on Tuesday evenings, hosting and leading a small group for church on Wednesday nights, preaching at the campus ministry meetings every Thursday night, attending campus outreach events on Friday nights, and preparing for all kinds of up-front responsibilities for church on Saturday evenings. We also had youth group meetings scattered throughout the calendar and various counseling sessions with couples, which Laura and I conducted together. As an overachiever, I'm quite sure I added a lot to my plate that wasn't being asked of me, but either way, the pace of it all was proving to be unrelenting and unsustainable. I had thrown myself into the hard work of pastoral ministry in a young and growing church with little consideration toward how to care for my own soul and our brand-new marriage.

It wasn't long before Laura and I were having regular fights on our dates, leaving us both irritated with one another as each new week approached. By the time we had crossed the two-year mark in pastoral ministry, I was completely burned-out. It seemed like every area of the church under my sphere of responsibility was doing well—except for me—and I was beginning to resent the ministry and the toll it was taking on me and my marriage. I felt lonely, isolated, exhausted, and utterly depleted. I was in a state of mental exhaustion and emotional turmoil when I walked behind a bookstore one day and cried out to God in prayer, saying, "Lord, if this is what ministry is like, I don't think I can do it. I'm so worn out. If You want me to do something else, please make it happen quickly." Two weeks later, I was called in to a pastor's meeting where I was informed by the pastoral team of our church that they had decided to release me from my position. Though I saw it as an answer to my prayers behind that bookstore, it was one of the most difficult and humbling experiences of my life.

In the coming days, it was communicated to the church that my transition from ministry was not a disciplinary action for a moral failure of any sort—that I had not been disqualified from ministry for any reason—but that based on the needs of the church and where I was as an individual in my professional experience, my employment there was no longer a good fit and the church would be releasing me to pursue another career. Regardless of how carefully it was communicated, I reeled with despondency and despair. Word quickly got out that I was no longer employed with the church, and my phone started ringing with offers for ministry positions in other areas, but I just couldn't bring myself to accept any other ministry opportunity.

In the end, Laura and I made the difficult decision to stay in the city we were in, continuing as members of the same local church that had fired me. I took a straight-commission sales job and started selling cell phones in the kiosk of our local mall. I felt like a colossal failure. I had lost my pay and my ministry influence in one fell swoop; it didn't just feel like a change of employment, but of calling and purpose. Nothing Laura would say could ease the sense of my own unworthiness. I had been fired from the church I loved, and since we chose to stay there, we daily felt the pain of it all. Sunday mornings were particularly hard, and Laura grew accustomed to me needing time on Sunday afternoons to retreat somewhere to pray. There was an abandoned construction site near our home where I would go regularly to cry, pray, and talk to God in the midst of all the emotional turmoil in my soul. Nothing else would soothe the pain.

Jesus used my failures to draw me close to Him. Yes, I was a failure, but I was *His* failure, and He took me in. Psalm 62:8 became a lifeline for me: "Trust in him at all times, O people; pour out your heart before him; God is a refuge for us." God invited me to share with Him everything going on in my heart and mind. Honest prayer became my form of trust. I did just what the text said—I poured my heart out, even all the nasty stuff, and talked with God about how deeply I was hurting. My prayerful anguish was like curdled milk draining out from a neglected carton.

I would be gone for hours and hours on a Sunday afternoon, lining the walkway of that abandoned construction site, drenching the ground with my tears, aware that I was completely by myself, but not alone. God was with me. Over time, I started looking forward to those Sunday walks. I thought often of a guy in the Bible named Enoch. Not much is written about Enoch, but if you ask me who I want to emulate in the Bible, it would be him. The Bible just describes him as a man who "walked with God" and someone who was commended as having pleased God (Gen. 5:24; Heb. 11:5). That's all I wanted—to walk with God and be commended as one who pleased Him. So, that's what I did. I literally *walked* with God and asked Him to help me please Him.

Though I had lost my ministry position, I hadn't lost His presence.

Slowly over time, even though my situation did not change, my perspective was transformed. I even began to thank God for allowing me to be released from ministry. That was such a hard prayer, y'all. I thanked Him for showing me that He didn't need *me* to accomplish His purposes and that I didn't need a ministry position to have a deep relationship with Him. I thanked Him for how He was using my humiliation to draw me closer to Himself, and I asked Him continually to strengthen my soul and my marriage.

Without all the pressures of ministry responsibilities, our calendar drastically opened up. Laura and I began to take long walks together. We found cheap restaurants we both enjoyed. We shared unhurried meals and late-night tears of solidarity. We discussed books we were reading. We dated; we traveled; we started loving each other again, deeply. God started to heal the brokenness from the first few years of our exhausted marriage. Processing the pain of failure brought us closer together, not further apart. I realized I had been such a jerk to Laura in our first few years of marriage. I had been so consumed with appearances and the desire to be well thought of by others that I was willing to be harsh with my wife to try to rally the control and respect I craved.

One day when Laura was gardening in our backyard, I noticed that our marriage was just like that garden—it needed to be tended with care, positioned in the sunlight, watered liberally, carefully weeded, and protected from predators. On a sheet of paper I kept in my Bible that I reviewed daily, I wrote out the first and second great commandments: to love the Lord your God with all your heart, soul, mind, and strength, and to love your neighbor as yourself (Mark 12:30–31). These commandments helped me simplify life. I wrote down the Scripture in Ephesians that says, "Husbands, love your wives" (5:25), and I wrote down what the Bible says love looks like—that it is patient and kind, it doesn't envy or boast, that it is not rude or easily angered, that it keeps

> **It took God breaking my own heart to give me a tender heart for the broken.**

no record of wrongs, that it always trusts, always hopes, always perseveres, that love never fails (1 Cor. 13:4–8).

I started seeing Jesus as a skillful, tender gardener. When people came to Him with all their burdens and their sins, He didn't set them on edge; He put them at ease. Jesus was so tender with His disciples. His very presence offered *rest* to weary souls (Matt. 11:28). That's why broken people flocked to Him. And He still offers rest to weary souls today.

I wanted to have this type of tenderness and care for my wife and for others.

It took God breaking my own heart to give me a tender heart for the broken.

Relieved from the external pressures of a ministry role, the church became such a solace for us again. In the midst of community, we healed. God provided true friendships marked by honesty, transparency, acceptance, and joy that strengthened us. We experienced the transforming power of being truly known and yet deeply loved, simultaneously. One of the pastors met with me monthly, cared for me masterfully, and listened to me patiently as I processed what God was doing in my heart. Our small group also cared for and carried us. I saw that the beauty of the church shines brightest against the backdrop of our own brokenness. I began to see that though being released from pastoral ministry was one of the hardest things I had walked through, God was using it for good in my life. The garden of our marriage began to thrive as we brought our brokenness to the One who could bear all our burdens. Echoing the sentiment of nineteenth-century preacher Charles Spurgeon, the same church that had fired me as a pastor once again became very, very dear to us:

Imperfect as it is, it is the dearest place on earth to us . . . for the church is not an institution for perfect people, but a sanctuary for sinners saved by grace, who, though they are saved, are sinners still, and need all the help they can derive from the sympathy and guidance of their fellow believers. The church is the nursery for God's weak children, where they are nourished and grow strong. It is the fold for Christ's sheep, the home for Christ's family.[1]

When my desires for ministry would not go away, I started praying a new prayer on my Sunday walks, "Father, if it's your will that I *return* to pastoral ministry, let it be that the team who released me would be the ones to bring me back." I asked God to demonstrate the power of His redeeming grace in this way, though that prayer felt to me like asking Him to part the Red Sea. Nevertheless, nearly five years after I had been fired, the same pastoral team that had terminated my employment extended me an offer to come back on staff at the church with the intent of being trained to help start another church in a different city. It was such a remarkable answer to prayer that after praying through it, I accepted the offer and rejoined the staff, giving thanks to God as a great Redeemer.

> *I saw that the beauty of the church shines brightest against the backdrop of our own brokenness.*

The church responded with joy as my reinstatement was announced. And about five years after that, the Lord opened the door for our family to relocate to the Nashville area to help start Redeeming Grace Church. Prior to the launching of this new church, we had the immense privilege of being part of Immanuel Nashville for nearly a year, where, sitting under the gracious ministry of a pastor named Ray Ortlund, I was comforted again regarding the failures of my past, while set free to dream big dreams again for Jesus. The Immanuel mantra was simple: "I'm a complete idiot; my future is incredibly bright; and anyone can get in on this." I resonated so much with this ministry, and it helped me envision what God could do with weary, broken-hearted failures who looked to Him alone for strength.

I vividly recall one morning when Ray said, "The three primary culture-shaping cities in the US today are New York, L.A., and Nashville. You are not here by accident. You didn't just show up in Nashville. God brought you here as a part of His strategy for world redemption."[2] I reflected often on that statement and prayed regularly, "Lord, please use me for Your glory; make my life like a finger pointing others to Jesus, the Great Redeemer."

The opening words at Immanuel repeated compassionately and graciously as a Call to Worship every Sunday morning were like waves of mercy lapping onto the shore of my soul:

> *To all who are weary and need rest;*
> *To all who mourn and long for comfort;*
> *To all who have failed and feel worthless and wonder if God even cares;*
> *To all who are weak and desire strength;*
> *To all who sin and need a Savior—*
> *This church opens wide her doors with a welcome from Jesus,*
> *the mighty friend of sinners,*
> *the ally of His enemies,*
> *the defender of the indefensible,*
> *the justifier of those who have no excuses left.*
> *You are welcome here.*[3]

You are welcome here. Yes, Jesus welcomes us in our mess, and He welcomes all the mess we bring with us; Jesus embraces sinners, sufferers, and people whose lives are in complete disarray. He says, "Come to me, all who labor and are heavy laden, and I will give you rest" (Matt. 11:28). Who doesn't need the kind of rest, comfort, care, and strength that Jesus promises? I know I do.

If you feel like a mess, I can relate.

If you feel like a failure, I am one too.

That night when Walker, Laney, and their family stepped through the doors of our church, I had no idea who Walker was professionally as a songwriter, but I immediately saw him as a new friend, and if I could do nothing else, I just wanted him to *feel* and experience the love and welcome of Jesus. Because through no merit of my own, it's a welcome I, too, have received. Indeed, it's a welcome that is available for all. For you.

We come to Jesus just as we are, or we don't come to Him at all. The good news is He doesn't care what kind of shoes you're wearing, and He doesn't mind if you spill your coffee.

3

DOG

CRAIG

WHEN MY OLDEST DAUGHTER, Karis, was eleven years old, she desperately wanted a dog. She asked us numerous times if we would be willing to get one for the family, and numerous times we told her, "Sorry, Love, we're just not a pet family."

We had come to this conclusion years prior while we were still living in east Tennessee, after reluctantly finding a new home for our over-hyper beagle named Charlie. Charlie was a great dog . . . until we had kids. Then, he must have felt dethroned, because he started acting up in every way imaginable: knocking our kids down, stealing food from little hands, shredding dirty diapers all over the floors of our home. These were just a few of the penalties among a host of other infractions that piled up against poor Charlie until we finally said "enough is enough" and found a new home for him with an elderly couple down the street. The couple was thrilled to have the company of our unruly beagle, our house became much more peaceful, and we were still able to visit with him from time to time until we moved to Nashville. Win-win-win.

Over five years later, my daughter was sweetly and consistently communicating a heartfelt desire to have another dog. The truth was, I *wanted* her to have her desire, but I also didn't want to go through what we had experienced with Charlie in the past. So, I thought hard about it, and at the dinner table one night I made a declaration:

"Baby girl, you are welcome to pray for a dog, but here's what would have to happen: It would have to be free (*because we're not going to buy a dog right now*). It would have to be hypoallergenic (*because your mommy is allergic to pet hair*). It would have to be housebroken (*because we're still trying to potty train a child and we're not going to add potty training a dog too*). It would have to be great with kids (*because we have four kids in the house*). It would have to be trained to be calm when people come over (*or crate trained, because we offer a lot of hospitality*), and we would need to have someone who is willing to watch the dog when we travel (*because we travel a lot*). That means it would probably have to be a labradoodle or something like that, good with kids, and given to us by someone willing to watch the dog when we travel. The odds aren't that great, sweetheart, but you're welcome to pray for it."

There it was. I had laid down the law, but with just enough room for an eleven-year-old to have specific requests to ask God to meet if the desire persisted. Karis took this list straight to the Lord. She prayed about it and began to appeal to God and others with her desire for a dog. Literally, she created a petition and took it to school and to church, asking people to sign it offering their support. It said something like, "I agree that Karis should have a dog." She even got my signature on the list, slyly asking to see the way I sign my name on a blank piece of paper (somehow, I ended up being the first signature!).

Several weeks later, Walker, Laney, and their kids were over for dinner at our house for the first time. As we were hearing their stories and the dynamics of their home life, Laney shared that they had two Goldendoodles back at their house, but they were considering a new home for one of them because they realized two dogs and five kids was too much. Laney said that the dog they would want to find a new home for, Tulip, was hypoallergenic, great with kids, housebroken, crate-trained, and they would even give her away for free if they could find a family who would love her. Laney must have seen the expression on my face as my eyes grew wide and my fork hovered in my hand. She must have sensed blood in the water because she started talking faster and excitedly said, "If *you* all want to take Tulip, *we'd even watch her for you whenever your family traveled.*"

Incredible.

Karis was sitting at the dinner table and heard it all. Who was I to argue with this apparently clear answer to prayer? Laney's statements checked off *every single stipulation* I had shared as a requirement for a dog. (And we hadn't even told Walker and Laney about the list I had given my daughter; we just said something like, "Yeah, Karis has been praying for a dog and begging us to get her one.") A little while after this dinner, Laney suggested to Laura that we take Tulip for "a trial weekend" to see how she matched with our family. I sheepishly agreed. Once we had Tulip in our home, the Cooper family immediately fell in love with her, and we decided to take her in as our own.

I was a bit blown away by all of this, but not completely surprised, as I've seen God answer prayers like this often. It felt like a supernatural cementing for what would become a very special friendship between our two families. Looking back, I see that Tulip wasn't just an answer to my daughter's prayers; she also was a means of grace in knitting the Hayes and Cooper families together. Both of our families traveled, often at the time, so we would regularly coordinate calendars for watching each other's dogs: Tulip from our house, and her sister, Magnolia (Noly, for short) from the Hayeses'. Drop-offs and pick-ups would inevitably turn into family gatherings, which we all eagerly embraced. All of our collective kids hit it off so well, Laney and Laura were becoming fast friends, and I loved every second I was able to spend with Walker. I realize it's a special bond when families mesh so well.

It's also amazing how God can use *anything* to accomplish His purposes. We see this all throughout the Bible. With Moses, God used a simple staff to perform miraculous signs and show His power, freeing the Israelites from Egyptian bondage (Ex. 4:1–5; 7:19; 8:5, 16; 14:16). God delivered David from the hand of Goliath with a little sling and a stone (1 Sam. 17:40). The modest offering of five barley loaves and two fish handed over freely from a boy was used by Jesus to feed a multitude of five thousand with leftovers to spare (John 6:1–14). And there's even a story in the Old Testament where God spoke through the mouth of a donkey (Num. 22:21–39)! Now, if He can speak through a donkey, He can certainly work through a dog; in our case, He used two sister-dogs, Tulip and Noly, to unite the Hayes and Cooper families together in the midst of all the unremarkable stuff of everyday life. Really, it was all so ordinary, but is there ever really anything ordinary when it's in the hands of an Almighty God? Psalm 24:1 says, "The earth is the LORD's and the fullness thereof, the world and all those who dwell therein." *Everything* on earth is God's, including the dog-stuff of our daily lives.

In addition to watching each other's pets, we spent time together at our kids' basketball and baseball games, with countless hours over dinners in each other's homes and in local restaurants. It became our rhythm to attend church together on Saturday nights. Walker typically stood outside the church building holding his youngest daughter, Loxley, until the end of the service, and then we would all go out to eat together at one of the Hayeses' favorite Mexican restaurants, which quickly became a favorite of the Coopers as well. Walker made it clear to us that he didn't believe in God the way we did, but for some reason, he kept coming back, and we all seemed to thoroughly enjoy each other's company, laughing and talking late into the night like we had known each other for all our lives. I sensed the smile of God on our friendship, and any amount of time together only made us hunger for more of their company. Our dogs are much to blame (or to thank) for the countless hours we've enjoyed in each other's homes.

WALKER

Tulip was the worst dog. The worst. Her sister Noly, on the other hand, is the perfect dog. Fat, lazy, dumb, and chill. Tulip was high strung, loud, and obnoxious ALL the time. She would jump up on every single person that entered our house, no matter what we did to try and break her of the habit. Tulip was a barker. Any noise would set her off. It's like she couldn't stop. If someone knocked at the door, she lost her mind. Like dry heaving but barking. She was an aggressive crotch sniffer. Tulip would just about lift me up off my feet with her nose when I came home. Given the right house, space, and time in our lives, I'd love to say we might have possibly appreciated her spunk, but nah . . . I would be lying. We just don't do dogs like Tulip.

What's weird is we had actually picked Tulip out of the litter. I remember the day we went to pick her up from the breeder, we were warned by a sweet family on their way out with their new puppy. They pointed to Tulip sleeping and said, "She's sleeping now, but you should have seen that one a minute ago . . . she was CRAZY!" We should have listened to them. That day, while picking up Tulip, I fell in love with this plump, sloth-like, lump of blonde fuzz that was Noly. She was by far the largest, most lethargic pup in the bunch. I begged Laney and then haggled the breeder for a two-for-one special. He should have given us Noly to take Tulip. We should have just bought the fat one.

Two dogs were too much for us, but we managed. "Too much" was just par for the course at that time in our lives. To be honest, I don't think Laney and I were actively looking for a home for Tulip. That would have been way too responsible of a decision to make, like only getting one dog in the first place. We would have just dealt with Tulip till she got old and died. When Craig mentioned Karis praying for a dog, I smiled like the Grinch to myself. I didn't believe in prayer, but that was the best one I'd ever heard. Laney and I could see the light bulbs blinking in each other's heads. It was perfect. Unloading Tulip this way almost made us look like heroes! I remember feeling the need to at least pretend I was a little bit sad when we gave her to them. Maybe I didn't. Truthfully, I can't remember if I was still "trying" around the Coopers or not. All I remember is that I was more than happy to say goodbye to Tulip.

It seemed like a pretty sweet deal from our perspective. After we gave them Tulip, we became mutually reliant on each other as dog sitters when our families would travel. Occasionally having to keep Tulip for the Coopers was the only downside. Whenever we had her, we were immediately reminded why we were so eager to find a new home for her in the first place. If one of our kids happened to accidentally leave a door open for too long, Tulip would bolt out of the house and never look back. It was a little bit embarrassing, constantly losing the dog we were supposed to be taking care of. We were always like, "How long should we wait until we call the Coopers and let them know their dog is missing?" Craig, if I've never told you this, I promise, we always found her pretty quickly. Our neighbors got used to returning Tulip to the brick house with a hundred kids. The only upside was that at least I could be like, "Hey, she's not my dog."

When we would hang at the Coopers' house, Tulip would bug me to death. It's like she thought I actually missed her. She would NOT leave me alone. She'd lick my hand, beg me to pet her, climb and jump all over me. If I was in the room, she was attached to me and refused to calm down. I remember acting nice like, "Aww, it's ok . . . Hey, Tulip, this is cute. What a great dog." . . . thinking to myself, "You stupid beast. I am so grateful you live here now." But my goodness, the Coopers loved that dog. She was a part of their family like their fifth kid or something. They actually *wanted* Tulip. Craig has a million pictures of her on his phone. I have zero. Tulip was the luckiest dog in the world. I mean, I was dumbfounded by the way they baby-talked to this aggravating excuse for man's best friend. It is incomprehensible how much they loved Tulip. Looking back, their love for me was the same.

At this point in our relationship with the Coopers, I would still refer to them as "Laney's friends." Lots of psychology that I can't explain going on there. Maybe I was mad at what they stood for. I thought it was all a crock. The whole Jesus thing. I felt separated from them because of their beliefs. At times, their spiritual connection with Laney and my kids made me feel separated from my own family too. In my head, I labeled myself the oddball in the group, yet in reality they never once considered me an outsider. Sometimes I would say, "Lane, we just saw the Coopers . . . can't we take a break?" Funny thing is, I actually enjoyed kickin' it at their house. It's like I hated that I loved having dinner with them. That's messed up, right? But get-togethers had to happen, whether I was in the mood for them or not . . . sometimes because of Tulip.

Tulip was just another unlikely path that connected me to Craig. An obnoxious, slobbering, bad-breathed, pushy, untamable, furry mistake of a path that made us bump into each other more often. She kept me around a family that was consumed by the love of God. Tulip forced me to walk with the Coopers when I didn't want to . . . which just meant I *had* to be accepted by them while I rejected myself.

4

WEDNESDAY

WALKER

A regular music gig is pretty difficult to find in Nashville since everyone and their brother sings and plays. And chances are, in Nashville, they are extremely talented. I remember going to my first open mic night at the Bluebird Cafe. I chickened out and snuck away before it was my turn when I realized everyone was playing their original material and I'd only prepared cover songs. Scary stuff. The only regular gig I had in Music City for the first five or six years was standing on the corners of Broadway, busking for bar-hopping people strolling by. Laney would drive me downtown on random Saturday nights and drop me off near Tootsies Orchid Lounge. I'd find a "quieter" spot between two bars, set up a music stand with lyrics to popular cover songs, and put my open guitar case beside me for folks to throw money in. I would make around a hundred bucks an hour! A little bit of alcohol can make a person *real* generous. It was a good experience, minus the cold nights and the occasional pigeon pooping from the rooftops. Thank goodness it never hit me, just the lyrics in my notebook.

So, after playing the "sidewalk" circuit for a few years, you can imagine how jacked I was when Andy Marshall, the owner of Puckett's Boathouse, graciously gave me the opportunity to play. The Boathouse was a little seafood restaurant located right next to the Harpeth River in downtown Franklin. It was a huge upgrade from the street corners of Broadway. There was a small stage in the corner of the restaurant seating, next to the kitchen hallway. I played one Wednesday for a couple hours while Andy checked in every now and then to see how it was going. Thankfully, people didn't boo or throw food at me, and Andy agreed to let me play for tips every Wednesday. Hence, Walker Wednesday was born.

Over time, Walker Wednesday evolved from just my acoustic guitar and me to a pretty tight three-piece band. The DeJaynes brothers elevated the evening many notches with their good looks and musical skills. Luke and his younger brother, Mark, loyally jammed with me for the better half of a year at the Boathouse. Luke played the drums and sang harmonies while Mark thumped the bass. Luke and Mark had no business being that committed to Walker Wednesdays. They could have both landed way-more-glamorous gigs in town, but for some reason, they stuck with me. We split a tip bucket that was maybe one hundred bucks on a great night.

There wasn't much to celebrate in my career those days, but for two hours every Wednesday, I completely forgot reality. We were rockstars at the Boathouse. We would set up at about 6:30 p.m. and have a few beers on the house. We would take the stage at seven and play about an hour-long set of mostly originals, with a few covers. Then, we would transition into an open mic night where random folks could get up and play with us. Oftentimes, cowriter friends of mine would come out and jam with us. Sometimes, complete strangers would show up to pick a little. My favorite was when I could convince my kids to get up with us and party. They always brought the house down! Lela, our oldest daughter, was famous for her version of "You're My Best Friend" by

Don Williams. With a little bribing, even Chapel and Baylor, the next two kids in age, would jump on stage and sing too.

Speaking of kids, the Boathouse took great care of ours. There was always a table reserved for Laney and our crew, and the food was free. There's no telling how many crab claws, popcorn shrimp, fish tacos, catfish fingers, and sweet potato fries the Boathouse fed us. They were family. The staff was so kind to our kids, forgiving of our mess and broken dishes, and always sent us home with a stack of to-go boxes.

While I indeed felt pretty dang famous walking in and out of the Boathouse every Wednesday, there was one humbling night I'll always remember. There was a couple whom I had never seen before sitting at one of the tables. I noticed the guy was singing along to my originals. This was an extremely rare sight from the stage those days because my career had already crashed and was only burning. But this stranger was singing along like I was Alan Jackson in the '90s. I had to go meet him during our break.

His name was Nick, and he was a die-hard fan of my stuff. He said a ton of flattering things about my writing. He was a singer and songwriter himself and joined the band for the open mic portion that night. Dude was amazing. After the show, he and I continued our conversation, and he grilled me for advice. I was feeling pretty great about myself, dropping words of wisdom about the biz to an adoring fan until he mentioned he worked in the tire center at Costco. I immediately snapped back to reality because the truth was, I needed a job.

We were struggling. Even though I got paid a draw to write songs and received additional income from playing gigs, I could hardly pay the bills. We had budgeted for all the basic necessities but didn't have anything left at the end of the month for emergencies. Laney remembers the kids asking for bagels at the grocery store and having to remind them that those were luxury items we couldn't afford. Career-wise, there was nothing on the horizon indicating our checking account would change anytime soon. We were running out of time and money.

So, I finally swallowed my pride and asked, "Nick, do you think Costco has any early morning job openings?"

He laughed and said, "Good one, man!" Then I shamefully watched his face go from smiling to George-straight as he came to the stark realization that I wasn't joking one bit.

Nick handled the awkward situation graciously and offered relief. "Costco might actually be looking for someone to stock the produce section from 4:00 a.m. to 10:30." Music to my ears.

At his request, I autographed his napkin. But my pride was shot.

As he left that night, he assured me, "I'll put in a good word for you with the boss."

Thanks to Nick, two weeks later, Costco hired me to stock the cooler five mornings a week. It was much-needed work, and the early hours allowed me to continue writing.

* * *

I've got Walker Wednesday memories for days. I'll never forget one Wednesday when we left the Boathouse to find one of our Accord tires had leaked flat during the show. At about 10:00 p.m. in the parking lot, our kids played Red Light, Green Light, while I replaced the right rear tire with the donut. Laney and I laughed because the donut looked about as flat as the flat tire did. That was us. After I loaded the flat in the trunk, she and I joined in the game with the kids and dominated some Red Light, Green Light! We laughed a lot. To keep from crying.

Another picture that will forever hang on the fridge of my mind is of Craig holding our little baby, Loxley. The Coopers were at Walker Wednesdays so often it's hard to imagine the Boathouse without them. Sometimes it was Craig, Laura, and their four kiddos. Sometimes, just Craig and Laura would pop in for dessert on a date night. And occasionally, it was just Craig. Regardless, a Cooper was always in the house. Craig held Loxley as naturally as I did. A portrait of Craig with a big ol' smile on his face holding her like she was his own would be the perfect album cover artwork for a record full of songs about how the Coopers did life with us. Their hands were dirty. They didn't watch from afar and just think about us or pray for us. They met us where we were. At the Boathouse. Among the noise, where the music wasn't "Christian," and the sound quality was sketchy. They gave us their attention and their presence. They had nothing to gain by knowing me, a starving artist with sharp edges and way too many kids. There was nothing in it for them. When you're a nobody in a town where it's all about who you know, it felt good that they wanted to know us.

Craig was my greatest hype man ever. Homeboy was always selling me and my music to some stranger beside him. Craig was, and still is, a shameless plugger of some Walker Hayes. He could have been my agent. If you ever met him at the Boathouse, I'm sure you got an earful of how amazing I was . . . and my personal favorite, like a broken record, he swore that I was destined to play stadiums one day.

Craig's wife, Laura, would always come in and join Laney and our circus of kids and do the chaos with her for a bit. Those two always seemed to just pick up where they last left off. Around Laura, I never got the feeling that Laney felt the need to try hard. And Laney wasn't really a "pass your kids around" type of mom. She was normally pretty particular about who held her babies, but somehow, Craig and Laura just made those walls come tumbling down. Same with the way they approached us with their own kids. We had grown accustomed to the "hide your kids" vibe we got from others we'd met. It was surprising how the Coopers joyfully met us in our mess with mercy.

CRAIG

ON WEDNESDAYS, OUR FAMILY WOULD sit with the Hayeses' while Walker performed original songs at Puckett's Boathouse. It was such a joy to see Walker in his element. Anywhere from fifteen to fifty people were seated in the restaurant at any given time. I was blown away by how gifted Walker was, and I was somewhat dumbfounded by the reality that he was performing for such a small group of people, many of whom were talking and not even listening to the music. It has been said that "music during dinner is an insult both to the cook and the musician." After weeks of what we affectionately came to know as "Walker Wednesdays," I adopted that sentiment as well. I just wanted everyone to stop talking, listen to the music, and appreciate Walker's gifting.

We stayed late after the shows, and once the restaurant closed, I'd stand with Walker in the parking lot encouraging him that I truly believed he'd be playing in stadiums one day. I received his music as a gift from God and soaked in every song. Privately, I would pray and ask the Lord to use Walker's gifts to one day draw people's attention to Jesus and even draw Walker himself to Christ through his own songs.

We progressed from spending Wednesday nights together to regular dinners throughout the week in each other's homes. Through countless meals together, we became more like family than friends. We started sharing everything together—the pain of the past, our hopes for the future. I found myself rooting for Walker's career and praying for him constantly, longing to have fellowship with my friend in Christ. I wanted him to know the Lord and experience His goodness the way I had.

What was amazing is that Walker encouraged me too. One day, he and I were golfing together, and I opened up about the details of my past, my family's past, and what God had done in my life. From then on, anytime I was scheduled to preach, he would communicate the strongest encouragement to me after the message, even though he was not a believer. At one point, I said, "Walk, I don't understand . . . You don't even believe the gospel, but you encourage me *every time I preach it.*" Walker said, "I know *you* believe it, and if it is true, it's the greatest news in the world, and everyone needs to hear it." Walker was increasingly feeling more and more like a brother to me.

Speaking of brothers, I'm an identical twin, and I often joke with my twin brother that he has the FBI on speed dial. Stuart has made a living in technology sales, but he's made a hobby out of politics and private espionage. So, when he and his wife Jenny returned from their honeymoon saying that they had eaten dinner with the Mafia, I couldn't wait to hear about it.

My brother and sister-in-law were bestowed a week-long cruise in the Caribbean as a generous wedding gift from our parents. If you've ever been on a cruise, you know three things about the dining experience: the food is incredible, you can have as much as you want, and you don't get to pick who you're seated with.

Stu and Jenny missed the first night's meal, so they didn't know what to expect as they were walking in looking for their assigned seats on the second evening. "Jenny, don't freak out, but I'm pretty sure we're about to eat with the Mafia," Stu said under his breath when he located their table number from across the room and saw what looked like a scene from *The Godfather*. As they approached, my brother introduced himself and his new bride, "Hey, everyone, we're Stuart and Jenny Cooper. It looks like this is our table."

"Honeymooners! So, *that's* why you weren't here last night," replied the man reclining with both arms resting on the back of his seat. "Sit down," he said forcefully, pointing his finger at the table.

Stuart pulled the chair back for his new bride as the man continued in a thick accent, "Sally, Frankie, Sue, and Al. We're from Jersey."

"Excuse me?" Stu asked.

"I said, 'Sally, Frankie, Sue, and Al.' That's our names."

"Oh, got it. Nice to meet you," Stu said.

My brother eyeballed the table, and noticed that Frankie, the man speaking, had sunglasses on inside the dining hall of the cruise ship, and his shirt was unbuttoned half-way, revealing large clumps of dark chest hair adorned by gold chains. Sally, who was clearly Frankie's wife, was dressed to the nines.

"So, what do you guys do for a living?" Stu asked.

Frankie answered for the table. "Al here sells baseball cards. *Ain't that right, Al?*"

Al looked like a younger version of Frankie, less confident, taking his cues from the man in charge.

"Yeah, that's right. I sell baseball cards."

Stu didn't skip a beat.

"That's awesome. I *collect* baseball cards. What do you sell?"

"What do you mean?" Al asked.

The guests at the table began to shift in their seats. Al recovered, "I sell Topps. That's right, Topps."

Just then, a waiter named Fernando interrupted the flow of the conversation and asked if they were all ready to order. The table started conversing individually, and Frankie interrupted:

"Forget about it. One of *everything* for everybody."

Then he directed Fernando over to his side, handed him a big wad of cash and said, "Fernando, you're a prince among men."

Stu looked at Jenny wide-eyed.

That night after dinner, Stu said, "They're gonna kill us, Jenny. They're gonna stuff our bodies in a refrigerator!"

But they were on a cruise for the first time, so they kept attending their dinners. After all, the food is great, you can have as many lobsters as you want, and you can't pick who you're seated with. Stu and Jenny made it every night, all the way to the final dinner when Frankie let out a big sigh and said, "This has been a great cruise. It's too bad we're gettin' indicted when we go back."

"What? You're getting indicted?" Stu asked. "What for?"

Sally spoke for Frankie, "They're babies. They're babies. They don't need to hear this."

Frankie said, "It's alright," and continued, "You know the luggage trucks at the airports?"

"Yeah," Stu said.

"We took a bunch of 'em."

"You stole them?" Stu asked.

"*Yeah*, we stole 'em."

"How many?"

"Eh . . . a lot of 'em."

"Oh."

Every time I hear this story, I can't help but laugh at Stu's uncommon encounters. It also makes me think of Jesus' unruly dining habits. If your view of Christianity is prudish and uptight, you may have the wrong Jesus in view. The real Jesus would eat at *that table*. Author Bob Goff wrote, "Most of us spend our entire lives avoiding the people Jesus spent His whole life engaging."[1] You may not realize this, but Jesus' first disciples were a ragtag crew. They were not from the polite corners of society, and they were not scriptural scholars. They included several fishermen, a tax collector, and an outspoken pessimist. They were ordinary, common men. They argued with each other often, but they were united by the desire to follow and learn from Jesus.

Jesus loved people so much that He was often accused of keeping questionable company (Luke 5:30). The accusations didn't alter His actions, though, as He kept welcoming sinners to dinner with Him. Jesus' response to the allegations was classic: "Those who are well have no need of a physician, but those who are sick. I have not come to call the righteous but sinners to repentance" (vv. 31–32). Jesus understood that a physician has to get close enough to the sick in order to bring any healing. Jesus is the Great Physician. He isn't concerned about external rules and regulations as much as He's concerned with healing the sick and caring for the bruised and broken. He's on a mission of mercy. So, it wasn't a chore for Jesus to spend time with unbelievers; it was His delight. Jesus made broken people feel comfortable in His presence. The truth is, we're all broken, but Jesus makes us feel at ease.

As Christians, we have the opportunity to do this too—to welcome people into Jesus' presence and make them feel at ease. When Christians fling their lives open wide, it's amazing how people can sense the love of God in the open arms of the Savior. They may not be able to articulate it, and they may not even understand fully what God is doing in those moments, but there's a sense of God that engulfs the living room, family life, and dining table of every open-armed Christian. What if we viewed what mattered most about our homes not as the decor or the financial value of the house, but the welcome it extends to the world in need of the love of God, the conversations and unburdening that can happen around the dining room table? Who is sitting there, what is being shared, what discussions and interactions and ministry are taking place in those moments—isn't that what matters most? As we're standing in the kitchen doing dishes together after dinner or sitting in the living room lingering over another cup of coffee, Jesus is at work. If Christ is in every Christian, doesn't it stand to reason that people will unwittingly encounter the life of Christ as we simply dine together?

As we discovered spending time with Walker and his family, genuine hospitality transcends the dinner table. The presence of Christ can be felt through us wherever we are, whether in our own home, at a restaurant, a pub, or a baseball game. The location is not what matters; we can extend Jesus' love and rest to anyone, anywhere in this restless world.

5

BAR

WALKER

Never stand on an empty trash can while catching a bed frame dropped from the second-story window of a house. I was helping Craig move, and I vividly recall it all going down—literally all going down—thinking, "I got it, I got it, wait . . . I don't." I hit the ground hard, but the drunk cushioned my fall as well as my embarrassment.

At the time, I was working early mornings at Costco. As soon as I clocked out, I'd drive to my shack on Music Row in Nashville, where I wrote songs for a small publishing company called RareSpark Media. Suzanne Strickland, the owner, and Scot Sherrod, the general manager, signed me as a writer when I didn't have a prayer. I had written for two publishing companies over the span of about twelve years and neither of them had made a dime off of me. RareSpark went out on a limb, and I was beyond grateful to have a writing family. Behind their building on 17th Ave. was a toolshed full of old junk, furniture, and lawn equipment. When they signed me, we emptied the shed out, cleaned it up, and called it the "Shack." I had some recording equipment in there, a couple guitars, and a couch. That's where I wrote and produced all of my songs. There was a small fridge in the basement kitchenette of the main building that I kept stocked with beer.

While trying to defibrillate a career in music that never really even had a pulse to begin with, my life revolved around my next drink. I would crack a beer around 11:00 a.m. as I sat down to write. Some days it was vodka in my coffee, other days it was whiskey, but most days it was beer. I would chain drink, with or without my cowriters, until I finished writing at about 3:00 p.m., and then I'd go to a bar called Mojo. My self-esteem was directly related to what I created, so if I felt like I'd written a hit that day, I drank to celebrate, and if I felt like I'd written a dud, I drank to forget the failure.

Sometimes I drank with the boys I'd written with that day, sometimes I drank alone. My favorite beers were with one of my best writer buddies, Jimmy Kup. He and I sat at the same table every day. I would typically drink at least four beers before I felt like it was time to close my tab. Some nights, Laney would call and catch me still there, way past four beers. She would always ask me how many I'd had, and I would always divide the truth by two and say that number. She just wanted to know I was okay, but I would laugh and say, "I'm fine, Lane, it's all good." I laugh when I lie.

I am terribly ashamed to admit I drove drunk on a daily basis. I learned where cops were and where they weren't. I knew which roads to take everywhere between Nashville and Franklin without passing one. After hanging at Mojo, I would head home or to play a show. I had a few weekly gigs at a handful of local bars and restaurants in addition to the Boathouse. The Bluebird Cafe and Gray's on Main were two of my go-tos. The owners of these places were so gracious to feed me and my family. Free drinks were a sweet perk as well. I'd throw a couple down before taking the stage and then I'd plow through them while performing, occasionally dropping a "Can I get a refill?" in the mic. My hand naturally reached for a glass between songs. I'm not sure I'd ever played a show completely sober in my life.

At the end of the day, I would eventually make it to our house in Franklin. If there wasn't any beer in the fridge or liquor in the cabinet, I would drive to the neighborhood grocery store, often with a beer between my legs. Sadly, I would invite the kids to ride with me. They knew my habits too well. As we walked down the beer aisle they would point to the cases of Blue Moon and say, "Daddy's beer." I would typically fall asleep on the couch with a bottle or glass in my hand. I would wake up sometimes and realize Laney had been sweet enough to pry it from my fingers before I spilled it in my lap.

The next morning my alarm would go off at 3:00 a.m. I would shower, eat a little something, then drive to Costco around 3:30 a.m. I remember being pulled over one morning knowing that I was still drunk enough to get a DUI. The officer just asked me where I was going and told me I had a busted headlight. My hands were shaking on the wheel as I finished the ride to work. On numerous occasions, in the Costco parking lot waiting to walk inside, I would pour a little something in my coffee for the pain. I always kept alcohol hidden in the console or under the seat. At about 3:55 a.m. I'd walk in the back door, punch the clock, throw on a jacket and some gloves, step in the freezer and start stocking celery.

Laney was so sweet. She would google things like, "Is my loved one an alcoholic?" regularly. This hurts to type. She was so scared and worried about me. Even though my drinking kept her up at night and negatively affected her life in so many ways, she was far more concerned for mine. Her motives were never selfish. Don't get me wrong, her compassion annoyed me sometimes, but that was just my pride bowing up. She just loved me and wanted to help.

She would calmly suggest, "Can we talk about it?" and I would not so calmly suggest, "Can we not?" I was tired of talking about it. Most of our conversations were the opposite of calm. They were laced with anger and frustration, but we communicated, nonetheless. For years we discussed my drinking and I repeatedly argued that I had it under control, but over time I began to cave and admit to Laney that I was indeed an alcoholic. I didn't need to google it. I confessed to her, "Yes, I have a problem, but I need that problem." I was afraid I couldn't perform sober; I was afraid I couldn't write sober, that I couldn't do life sober. I was completely at the mercy of my addiction.

I despise what I put Laney through. I know what it's like to love someone who is killing themselves, and it is a painfully helpless feeling. The only thing worse is knowing I made Laney feel like that for a long, long time. Regardless, Laney loved me through it all and never left, even though I chose alcohol over her, our kids, and my own life for many years. One of the saddest nights of my life was when Laney tearfully presented me with information describing a long-term rehab center she had found for me. That was when I realized how low I'd sunk.

It took a while for that knowledge to change my destructive patterns, and in the meantime, I created new drinking appointments to cut the edge. McCreary Monday started with two people, me and another creative type. Just two dudes at McCreary's Irish Pub having a few. We had similar taste in music and spent most of our beers worshiping the sounds of our heroes and knocking the noise we were jealous of. We gave our meeting the name, "McCreary Monday." I mentioned it to a buddy who ran sound at Puckett's Boathouse, Jonathan Thatcher. Rockstar. I mentioned it to a neighborhood bud, John Mallory, also a rockstar. They both joined us. Craig and his brother Stuart were early members of the gang too. It wasn't long till we were having to put tables on the ends of tables to make it large enough to fit everyone that showed up. McCreary Mondays became a thing.

The group was eclectic, but the table quickly became lopsided with men from Craig's church, Redeeming Grace. Craig is a recruiter. How could I expect anything different? That's what he does for a living. Dave, their head pastor, and Seth, one of their worship leaders, would frequently join. Over time, I began to notice one of these chairs was not like the others. All these dudes loved Jesus, and I didn't believe in Him. I found it pretty funny that I had basically started a men's group. Being the manipulator I am, I used the "Redeeming Gracers" as leverage when Laney would hit me with the "Where have you been's?" and "How many have you had's?" She loves church, so how could she argue with "I've been hanging with the preachers"?

However, as the McCreary Monday crowd grew, the conversations grew richer. I'm not really a "band of brothers" guy, and I'd originally started the party as a way to keep my buzz going a little longer, but every Monday, I found myself looking forward to hanging with the brothers more than I did the beers. What was revolutionary to me was that these men loved the Lord, knew I didn't, and still chose to join me on my turf to catch up on life, talk music, kids, baseball, football—to just listen and be heard. That's another thing, I wasn't the "project" at the table. They valued my input and presence at the table even though I didn't ask God to bless my beers. It's like I was the woman at the well and the well was McCreary's and Jesus was in their hearts.

I'm not sure if Dave will even remember this, but one night he asked me something personal. I can't even remember what he asked me, because I'm sure I was hammered, but I remember coming dangerously close to ugly crying in McCreary's trying to formulate an answer. I'm guessing it was something about my family. I was surprised by how comfortable I was to get into such a vulnerable conversation. That wasn't me. I didn't share inside information with anyone other than Laney. I remember thinking as I left, "I gotta start drinking a little later on Mondays so I can keep my stuff together."

Though I cannot recall the memory, Craig guarantees, without a doubt, that one night I said, "I'd believe there is a God if I could quit drinking." It sounds like something I would say in my head but not out loud, but the fact that I did say it to Craig proves that I trusted him. Sadly, it had been a long time since I had done that, trusted someone.

One Saturday in October 2015, I woke up and couldn't drink. I literally couldn't. My body was dying from lack of sleep, working early mornings, playing late shows, and the constant drinking on top of it all. I truly felt like if I repeated one more day of my normal routine I might not wake up. So, I didn't drink. This was during football season, which was pretty unreal to consider since I'd probably been drunk every single Saturday in the fall since the tenth grade. I felt so great Sunday morning that I didn't drink that day either. A weekend turned into a week and a week turned into a month and so on. Years have passed now, but it has not always been easy. I have had tough days and nights where I have come dangerously close to backsliding, but I truly believe the prayers of my family and friends were answered. There is no other explanation.

I quit going to McCreary Mondays and it dissolved over time. One of the greatest witnesses to me was when one of those "Redeeming Gracers" I'll call Ralph hit me up one day asking how I quit. Apparently, he too struggled in the drinking department and reached out to me, a nonbeliever, for counsel in this area. To hear this believer's repentant heart and for him to humble himself to the point of asking me for help was so disarming. By the grace of God, I am so thankful to report he is now several years sober too! We check up on each other regularly.

I am grateful for this ugly part of my testimony. Since I quit drinking, I have had the privilege of walking mighty close with some fellow alcoholics who were inspired by what the Lord has done to me and watched them taste true freedom from addiction. I get goosebumps anytime anyone approaches me wearing their own vices on their sleeve because I know it is a giant step to admit a total loss of control. I want to tell the world of my relief and my true relief is Jesus Christ. I am humbled that He ate and drank with sinners, and I am thankful Craig did too.

I'm smiling while I type this. My buddy Jimmy Kup quit drinking about a year after I did, and he recently visited Redeeming Grace. The path was a bar.

I wrote a song about my freedom from the grip of addiction.

"Daddy's Beer"
Walker Hayes

I used to drive drunk down to Kroger
With my little girl in the backseat
How I never got pulled over
Is still a mystery to me . . .
We'd go walking down the beer aisle
Like we will on her wedding day
I remember she would stop & smile when she got to the Blue Moon & say . . .
Daddy's beer, daddy's beer
I'm sad to say she would but I can still hear her

(Chorus)
5 years since I've tasted a drop of alcohol
I don't feel like getting wasted & that's Jesus' fault
Yeah, He turned water into wine but tonight I'm sippin' proof
But He can turn wine into water too . . .
Just ask my daughter
He can make old fathers new . . .

Still have moments, still have seasons
Still more sinner than I am saint
I still wrestle with my demons and the reasons that I drank
But I know how I got home
& Who I'm saved by the grace of.
Nah, my daughter's not the only one that's done some growin' up since the
days of . . .

Daddy's beer, Daddy's beer
Now it's all a blur to her but my memory's clear

(Chorus)

I went down to the river & I got drenched
Ain't nothin' holy in my cup but my thirst is quenched . . .[1]

CRAIG

DURING THE TIME that we were all enjoying Walker Wednesdays, Walker sent out an invitation to a large group of guys, inviting us to what he dubbed "McCreary Monday." McCreary's is an Irish pub located directly off Main Street in downtown Franklin. It was a short two-minute walk from the old firehouse utilized by the company I worked for at the time. Each Monday, I looked forward to walking over to McCreary's to join Walker and a crew of songwriters, musicians, and friends for a time of laughter and connection. It was an eclectic group, and I loved it.

McCreary's has this rectangular shotgun-style outlay, with room for maybe thirty people at a time. Typically, the McCreary Monday crew held most of its occupants on those afternoons. Walking into the pub, you just feel as if you've been transported into the heart of Dublin. St. Patrick's Breastplate prayer spans across the entire frame of the ceiling, offering an ode from the Irish patron saint:

Christ with me, Christ before me,
Christ behind me, Christ within me,
Christ beneath me, Christ above me,
Christ at my right, Christ at my left . . .
Christ in the heart of every man who thinks of me,
Christ in the mouth of every man who speaks to me,

Christ in every eye that sees me,
Christ in every ear that hears me.[2]

I smiled every time I walked in and saw that message on the walls, reading it to myself in an Irish accent. I met *so many incredible people* during our McCreary Monday gatherings that I left each Monday afternoon with a huge grin on my face, thinking, *This is why we moved to Nashville.*

I believe we all crave community, a sense of belonging. The '80s–'90s show *Cheers* captured this desire so well in their theme song—"Sometimes you want to go where everybody knows your name, and they're always glad you came."[3] I can still hear that song playing in the background of my mind from when my parents watched the show in our living room when I was a kid.

McCreary Monday was more than a social gathering for me. It represented the realities of that Irish prayer and blessing that graced its walls. I was experiencing it in real time. Christ on my right. Christ on my left. Community. Belonging. Shared troubles and joys. A sense of togetherness. Brotherhood. Knowledge and love intertwined.

No one was trying to impress the other. We were just being real.

I loved every second of it. And Walker was the one who started it.

I honestly didn't realize Walker had a drinking problem until after he quit drinking. I never knew him any different. Now that I look back and think about it, he always had a beer in his hand, but there was only one occasion when I thought he might have been inebriated.

It was the night we were moving houses. Walker pulled up to the house alone, there to help us move. My friend Adam and I were upstairs trying to figure out the best way to get the kids' bunk beds out the door and into the moving trucks when Walker joined us and suggested we lower them out the window. Walker was stumbling a little bit but offered to be the one to grab ahold of the beds on the receiving end as we hoisted them down.

Adam and I chuckled as Walker realized he couldn't reach the beds we were lowering, so he positioned our grey trash can just under the window, climbing on top of it with both arms outstretched. Well, the trash can completely flipped out from underneath him, and he fell down the side of the hill! That was a pretty good indication. We were all doubled over with laughter and thankful he hadn't injured himself in the fall.

I soon learned that Walker would begin drinking during his early morning writing sessions and continue throughout the day, ending in the evening at a bar. Sitting at his kitchen table, Walker said to me and Laura one night, "I would believe there's a God if I could quit drinking."

So, Laura and I started praying that God would take away his desire for a drink.

Walker stopped coming to McCreary Monday, stopped performing for Walker Wednesdays, and could no longer hang out late at night. The drinks stopped, too. He was just so tired and had to get in bed early to get enough sleep before his alarm sounded at 3:00 a.m.

Though he stopped drinking, he kept writing. He poured his heart out in lyrics that were honest and raw. He had lost a record deal and had hit rock bottom. So, he was no longer writing for Nashville or anyone else, just himself. Even if no one else would hear it—what came out of his pen was pure gold.

He wrote a song called "Beer in the Fridge" about his struggles with alcoholism and the effect it would have had on his life and marriage if he hadn't given it up. That song got picked up by The Bobby Bones Show, a massively popular syndicated radio show, and a glimmer of hope was sparked again for Walker's music career. As Walker has opened up with honesty and vulnerability about his struggles with alcohol, it helped me want to open up about my own failures and struggles too. There are parts of my life that for years I wanted to keep hidden and undisclosed as I've struggled with my own sense of shame (like getting fired from pastoral ministry), but having a front-row seat to the transformation I've seen in Walker's life has made me want to be more vulnerable as well.

I think we all have that middle-school-kid tendency to hide. It's profoundly within us, down to our very core. We try to avoid conversations with the perceived authorities in our lives. We pull our shades. We close our curtains. We shut the garage doors of our homes and our hearts all too quickly at times. We work hard to conceal anything that makes us feel a sense of shame.

Trying to *hide* was the first thing Adam and Eve did after they ate of the tree God had commanded them not to eat from. But the truth is you can't really hide from God. He is omniscient, which means He knows everything. He knows who we are, what we've done, what thoughts we're having, and even what we're going to do in the future. His all-knowingness is a part of His nature as God. The psalmist asks God, "Where shall I flee from your presence?" (Ps. 139:7). The answer is nowhere. So, if God already knows the state of our homes and our hearts, wouldn't it be best to just be honest?

Walker's honesty is one of the many things I have always respected about him. If honesty is an aspect of humility (which I believe it is), and God gives grace to the humble (which I believe He does) (James 4:6), perhaps Walker's honesty with his struggles was a big part of what would set him up to receive great grace in the days to come. I want to be more like him in that way. Walker's transparency about his struggle with alcohol was huge.

Now, I know that Jesus turned water into wine (John 2:1–12), and I believe there will be amazing wine in heaven the likes of which no vineyard in this world could compare (Matt. 26:29). I also know that if my brother struggles with alcohol (or anything), I'd rather abstain from it out of love to preserve my relationship with him (Rom. 14:20–21). It was a joy to share beers with Walker in the early days, and it was a joy to stop sharing beers with him when he decided it was best for him to quit drinking. I love my friend, and we didn't need a drop of alcohol to have a taste of friendship.

When Jesus walked on this earth, He connected to people in a way that they felt like He knew them . . . and still loved them. Isn't that what we all want? To be known *and* still loved? One of my favorite stories in the Bible is the moment when Jesus was talking to a woman at a well. It's recorded for us in the fourth chapter of the Gospel of John. The scene is set in the noon-day sun, the peak of the day's heat. Jesus, a Jewish man, was sitting thirsty and alone by a well when a Samaritan woman approached to draw water. Normally, the women of the area would have come in the early morning or evening to draw water from the well, as it was cooler then. This woman came at a time when no one else would be there—high noon. Scripture doesn't tell us the exact circumstance, but the implication for the original readers of this story is that this woman was not just an outcast of society, but an *outcast among outcasts.*

Jews of the time had no dealings with Samaritans and instead held them in contempt. They even tried to find paths of traveling that kept them from even interacting with Samaritans. But here, Jesus is in Samaria, initiating a private conversation with a Samaritan woman in the open air of a secluded water well. This would have been perceived by any onlooker as scandalous, yet there is so much empathy and compassion in this moment. Jesus addressed the woman kindly and asked her for a drink. The woman was absolutely astounded that Jesus would even speak with her. She said, "How is it that you, a Jew, ask for a drink from me, a woman of Samaria?" (John 4:9). You can almost picture the care and concern on Jesus' face as He says, "If you knew the gift of God, and who it is that is saying to you, 'Give me a drink,' you would have asked him, and he would have given you living water" (v. 10).

The woman pushed back, challenging Jesus a bit, and that's when Jesus said, "Go, call your husband, and come here" (v. 16). When she said she didn't have a husband, He told her He knew that she previously had five husbands and that the man she was currently with was not her husband. At this point, the Samaritan woman recognized Jesus as a prophet and began talking to Him about the coming Messiah. Jesus responded, "I who speak to you am he" (v. 26).

Yes, Jesus claimed to be the Messiah, the Savior of the world.

What's incredible is that by the end of their conversation, this woman felt accepted by Jesus even as she was fully known by Him. She ran away in joy, sharing with all the people, "Come, see a man who told me all that I ever did. Can this be the Christ?" (v. 29).

It doesn't matter who you are or what you've done; Jesus will draw near to have a drink with you, if you will have a drink with Him.

He already knows everything about us, and He loves us anyway. That's amazing love.

And if you ask *Him* for a drink, He'll give you living water, and as you will drink from the water of life, you will find that it is a well that never runs dry.

6

VAN

WALKER

During the time I was signed at Capitol Records, Laney and I had our third and fourth children, Baylor and Beckett. We had outgrown my old Honda Accord. But thankfully my management team had connections with a Volkswagen dealership in Texas. My manager was able to use my record deal and so-called "bright future" as leverage to entice them into loaning us a van. This was nuts! Music was far from paying the bills, but this perk didn't hurt. The owner of the dealership had high hopes that I'd be a household name any minute. They would use my face and my music in jingles and advertisements, and in return, we got whatever van we wanted that year. My kids loved guessing what color I would bring home each time I made the trip to and from Lewisville. The last one we had was white.

Around 2012, Capitol Records merged with Universal. This was the second time I had been through the old "label is moving in a new direction" wringer, and I knew too well that when this happens, a handful of artists are always lost in the shuffle. That's just the way it is. I could see it coming a mile away. However, when they finally kicked me to the curb, I couldn't really argue with their decision. I didn't look great on paper. They had invested four years and thousands of dollars trying to get me on the radio, and only one of my songs had barely touched the top 40. I wasn't the smartest investment. And, to be completely fair, I was my own worst enemy. I more than frequently butted heads with the team there. They did all they could for me and, in return, I was nothing but stubborn and un-coachable. A common sentence in the story of my life.

It was no surprise at all when my manager called to inform us that I was no longer an artist on their roster. It cut me deep, but I was holding the knife. There was no one to blame but me.

I knew the moment the Volkswagen dealership heard the news of my recently lost record deal they would no longer see the merit in loaning us a van. I was able to keep it a secret until Laney had Loxley, our fifth kid. I mean, sincerely, I would have loved to become famous overnight somehow without a label and reward the dealership for their early faith in me, but the fact is, I was just lying to them by hiding that I had been dropped. I remember finally feeling guilty and telling them over the phone. They didn't take it away immediately, but after a week or two, they called back and scheduled to come pick up the van.

Laney, the kids, and I watched at the entrance to our neighborhood as a semi-truck loaded it with the other cars that were already stacked up. My kids thought it was so cool. I mean, it was pretty cool. It's mesmerizing how they neatly pack so many vehicles on a semi, but it would have been way cooler if it had been someone else's van. I remember that hurt just about every single time I drive by our old neighborhood. I had no answers to the empty space in our garage.

I had gotten us into a pretty tough situation. The "us" part was what I struggled with the most in the whole chasing-a-dream thing. My own desperate circumstances are easy to shoulder, but when I've dragged my entire family into a pit, that's when I wanted a drink the most. I didn't know what to do and just kept saying, "I'll figure something out," but I never could. Laney and I were down to one car, our shared 2003 Honda Accord that was pretty ratty. The AC was long gone. The driver's side window wouldn't roll up and down. The back driver side taillight was just a ton of red tape peeling off, blowing in the wind, and the back passenger side tire was a donut.

Sharing a car was tricky at times. We taught the kids to duck down at red lights since there weren't enough seatbelts. Laney was a good sport and really let me use it most of the time. She homeschools all of our kids, so she didn't need the car until about 4:00 p.m. every day in order to run to gymnastics or baseball practices. I was still stocking produce at Costco and took extra shifts in the bakery as often as I had time. I'm not sure how much money we had in the bank, but we were definitely not able to afford a reliable second vehicle. Our first one wasn't even dependable.

Craig and Laura were kind enough to let us borrow their van from time to time. When we didn't have their van, a friend named Ray Boone would loan us his truck. This went on for a month or so while I chased my tail looking for a Band-Aid to stop the bleeding. Problem was, the car was just one out of a dozen problems that kept me staring at the ceiling fan every night. Our house was reaching the age where every single appliance was dying. Our kids were in more activities than we could afford. My career was disappearing. My license plate should have said FAILURE on it. One night my son Baylor had a baseball game. Just a regular weeknight experience for us all. The ballpark is a pretty peaceful place for me. The smell of burgers from the concession stand and the sounds always take me away from the reality of adulthood for a moment. When the game was over, our bunch wandered over from the bleachers to where the team met and then toward our car. I was surprised to see Craig standing in the parking lot. I just guessed Laura had heard from Laney that we were at the fields, and he'd decided to drop by. So, I walked up and said, "What in the world are you doing here?"

Craig was standing next to his Chrysler Town & Country van with a giant grin on his face. He was holding a piece of paper in one hand and pen in the other.

"All you have to do is sign and it's yours." I did the math in my head and began to figure out what was going on. I also noticed Laura was parked next to us in their other car, smiling. Laney and our kids stood there in disbelief as they realized what the Coopers were offering. The paper in his hand was the title to his van, and he'd even thought ahead, in Craig fashion, and provided a pen for me to sign it with. I should have been the happiest person in the park, but I wasn't. I was furious. I hated the situation, I hated myself, and I wasn't too happy with Craig either. I am embarrassed and ashamed to confess how ungrateful I was. Humiliation overwhelmed me. I couldn't believe it had come to this. I didn't want to need to be rescued. I was so deep in denial of how desperate I really was that I refused to accept the car. I told Craig, "No way, there's no way I'm letting you give me a car." I would not surrender to charity.

Craig and Laura all but begged me to take the van. I shook my head in defiance. My kids were saying, "Dad, just take the car!" I refused and refused, steadily pulling the mood of the moment from somewhat playful to almost awkward and tense, but then Craig said something that I desperately needed to hear. He said, "Hey man, somebody did this for me once. Just let me do this for you." Those words softened me. Those were the words that tapped my heart on the shoulder, turned me around, and invited me in. It was his empathy that gave me permission to acknowledge my own weakness. I continued to pretend I was putting up a fight, but I eventually signed the paper and drove the

> **It was his empathy that gave me permission to acknowledge my own weakness.**

van home. I got a little emotional when I noticed in the rearview that all the kids were buckled up.

I don't know if I'll ever fully process what actually happened that night. Craig wasn't wealthy. This was no small financial sacrifice for his family to make. They were able to replace their van with something used with decent mileage, but it wasn't like he could turn around and buy a brand-new Range Rover. Also, Craig wouldn't tell a soul about giving us the van. Even his twin brother, Stuart, had no idea for the longest time what they had done. Craig did everything in his power to keep it hush, but the Lord had other plans. Nice try, Craig.

CRAIG

WE KNEW THE HAYES FAMILY intimately by this point in our friendship, so it was no secret to us when they lost their van. Walker had even tried to negotiate an agreement with another dealership by writing an amazing song he thought they could potentially use in a commercial, but there was no deal to be made. We were close enough friends to know when the tow truck was sent to their house while their entire family stood outside watching as the van they had relied on was impounded.

Laura and I knew Walker and Laney were hurting, and we were hurting with them, even if the Hayes kids were young enough to think the whole impounding of their van was a fun event. I knew what it was like to struggle financially. A prayerful excerpt from my journal just a few months prior reveals that Laura and I were living paycheck to paycheck in that season ourselves:

We currently have $39 in the checking account and $249 in savings. My paycheck is to come tomorrow, but in any case, this is dangerously low. So, I can be anxious about our finances. Father, You know all my needs even before I ask for them. You know the sacrifices we've made and the financial setbacks we've encountered to go into full-time ministry for nearly eight years before moving to help plant a church. I feel like we're always scraping by. Father, please provide for us, according to Your Word and Your promises; please give us wisdom financially, please help us to "make up for lost time"; please deliver us from debt; please provide for us plenty so we have savings; please provide so I have more than enough and can leave a future inheritance to my children's children; please bless my work so I can be a blessing to my family, my church, and the world; and please give me the fear of the Lord, so my heart remains humble and generous even when big financial blessings come. Lord, I cast all these cares and concerns and anxieties to You, and I entrust my financial state—and future—to You, the One who owns it all and who knows my needs better than I do. My life is Yours. My finances are Yours. My work, my family, my all is Yours. "When I am afraid, I put my trust in you" (Ps. 56:3).

Below this entry, I penned a quote from a devotional called *Beside Still Waters* which reads: "Listen, child of God, you can lose your possessions, but you cannot lose your God . . . you may lose your savings, but not your Savior."[1]

In answer to those prayers, God provided just enough commission from a few closed deals at work to allow us to pay off our debt and have a little left over. The timing of it all was remarkable. I told Laura that I felt compelled to give the Hayeses' our family van. Laura completely agreed and said, "That's exactly what I was thinking." So, we started looking for a used vehicle to replace our van. I told a few friends I worked with that we were looking for a new family vehicle, though I didn't explain why. My friend Chad came back from a bike ride one day and mentioned he saw a used Chrysler Pacifica for sale down the street. I immediately went over there, test drove it, and asked the owner if I could take it to my mechanic for an inspection. Once everything checked out, Laura and I bought that car. With our new family vehicle intact, we began making plans to give our van to the Hayeses.

Laura nonchalantly found out from Laney that their son Baylor had a baseball game at a local park one evening that week, so we decided to surprise them there with the van. That night, I spent time cleaning the van and gathering the paperwork, so we didn't make it in time to actually see the ballgame. Walker was understandably surprised when he saw our family at the ballpark at the end of the game. "What in the world are y'all doing here?" he said smiling as we met them in the parking lot. It was dark outside, and our faces were barely illuminated by the stadium lights.

"We just got a new car and want you guys to have our van." I handed him the keys and the title. "All you've got to do is sign, and it's yours."

"No, *no way*," Walker said, taking a few angry steps back with his hands raised.

"Look, man, we don't need the van anymore. We're all set with our Pacifica, and we really *want* your family to have this."

"Craig, I can't take this. No way. You're crazy."

"Here's the title, bro. I've already signed my portion. Just take it, *please*. You guys can drive the van until something better comes along. It's yours now."

"No, Craig. I can't. I'm not taking your car." Walker replied with growing aggravation.

"Look, man, somebody did this for us once. Please, just let us do this for you."

Our two families saw the tension unfold like they were watching a movie, and then Walker's daughter Lela blurted out, "Dad, just take the car!"

That's when I started smiling. Walker teared up, reluctantly took the keys and the title, and gave me a hug. I could tell he was still a bit upset. We didn't say much else. We all just parted ways.

On the way home I said to Laura, "I hope I didn't offend him. I do think it's the right thing, and I just hope that van serves their family as much as it's served ours."

Then I turned to the kids. "Kids, listen, the Bible tells us, 'When you give, don't let your right hand know what your left hand is doing, so that your giving may be in secret.' So, we're not going to talk about this with anyone, not even Uncle Stu or Auntie; and we don't want you guys to share this with anyone else either. This is between us, the Hayeses, and the Lord. Do you understand?"

"Yes, Daddy."

* * *

I was about twenty years old when I first met "Pop," Laura's grandfather. A World War II vet, Pop had served with the US Army Eighth Air Force in Europe from 1942 to 1945. He was a member of the Greatest Generation, and his very presence in a room commanded attention. He was never intimidating—it wasn't like that—but Pop had an influence that was palpably felt in every family interaction where he was present. Dinners in Laura's childhood home were unlike anything I was ever accustomed to. The family would linger long at the table, sometimes sitting for an hour or more after a meal was consumed, just to talk and hear stories from Pop. It was during these many family dinners that I heard Pop talk about his youth, of growing up during the Great Depression, of running away to join the carnival as a teenager for weeks before one of his brothers found him and brought him home. I heard about family pranks and short-sheeting the beds of guests, and the time when a few cousins picked up the bed of one of their relatives at the beach and put it outside on the roof while he was sleeping. I heard about numerous emergency calls Pop took as a local fire station chief in Montgomery County, Maryland.

I could listen to all those stories a thousand times without ever getting tired of a single one. I admired Pop greatly. One time when I couldn't afford reliable transportation (I had bought a truck for $800 and ran it to the ground to the point that it was falling apart), he and I stood alone beside his Ford Ranger sitting idly in the detached garage of his farmhouse in Maryland, and Pop handed me the keys to the truck, with a pen and the title in his hand and said, "I want you to have this. All you've got to do is sign and it's yours." At that moment, this World War II vet, former fire chief, and true gentleman provided me with a picture of the gospel of grace. Pop gave me freely what I could not afford, and all I was asked to do was receive it.

When Jesus was asked by someone, "'What must we do, to be doing the works of God?' Jesus answered them, 'This is the work of God, that you believe in him whom he has sent'" (John 6:28–29). People want to know what they have to *do* in order to be right with God. We want lists. We want the twelve-step programs. We want something, *anything*, that will give us a sense of accomplishment and achievement to show that we have somehow earned good standing with God. But Christianity is not about what we must do, *it's about what God has done.*

The most well-known verse in all of the Bible speaks to this: "For God so loved the world, that he gave his only Son, that whoever believes in him should not perish but have eternal life" (John 3:16). Believing in Jesus—trusting in Him fully—is what opens the door to eternal life. And it is a gift. That's why Jesus says the work of God is that you *believe.* Salvation is a gift of grace that comes through the perfect life and sacrificial death of Jesus. If we think we have to earn it, salvation will never be ours. But if we can for a moment stop all the arguing and justifying of ourselves in our own minds long enough to simply embrace the beauty and the glory and the wonder of the gift of God, we will see that God freely gave what we could never earn. God owns the title to everlasting life, and He offers it freely to all who *believe* in Jesus. All you've got to do to receive salvation is sign the title—*believe*—and it will all be yours. Jesus lived a perfect life and then paid the full price for our redemption through His death on the cross on our behalf. Ultimately, any sacrificial love we show for one another on this earth is simply an echo of the kind of love God has for us in giving us His Son. Jesus already paid for it all—our peace has been purchased by Him.

> *Any sacrificial love we show for one another on this earth is simply an echo of the kind of love God has for us in giving us His Son.*

I'm not sure either Walker or I realized the significance of what was taking place as I handed him the keys and title of our family van that night in the parking lot of a dimly lit ballfield, yet God was powerfully at work demonstrating His love for both of us through a modern-day parable of the gospel of His grace.

You can't earn God's favor, but you can receive it. All you've got to do is sign—believe in Jesus—and it's yours.

7

A
SONG

WALKER

I could write a whole book's worth on a guy named Shane McAnally. The CliffsNotes version is he's the most gifted songwriter and producer Nashville's ever known. One Costco morning, I found myself in Smoothie King standing in line behind "The Real Shane McAnally!" Normally, I didn't wanna be that guy, but I was desperate, so I awkwardly tapped his shoulder and introduced myself. I stammered through the saga of my career woes and asked—begged—"Would you mind if I shared a song or two with you?" I still can't believe he gave me his actual email address. I knew I came on strong, but Laney was pregnant with our sixth child, Everly, and we were hurting. For the next ten months, I sent Shane a song every week; and for some reason, he continually shared them with the artists he worked with. Unfortunately, none of them recorded anything of mine, but I could feel the faith he had in me via email. It was incredibly kind of him to listen to my material because I know how high in demand he was. Jake Owen was the closest I came to having an artist release one of my songs through Shane. Jake actually recorded one I'd written called "Song In Your Pocket," but sadly and par for the course, it didn't make it on the album. My stuff was just out of the box. One Saturday in November, shortly after I'd gotten sober, Shane called me. I'll never forget it. I was walking home from the gym, and he was standing at his gate in the Nashville airport, about to board a plane.

"Walker, I'm tired of trying to convince other artists to record your songs. They just aren't responding. I still believe in what you are writing. Why don't we just make *your* album?"

I stopped and stood still on the sidewalk. I couldn't believe it. Shane McAnally wanted to produce a *Walker Hayes* album. I can't really remember the rest of the conversation, but I do remember running the rest of the way home to tell Laney. We cried together. A lot. I was quickly added to a ridiculously talented roster of writers at Shane's publishing company, SMACKSongs, and was able to officially retire from Costco about two months later. RIP Costco career.

So, fast forward to about a year later. My album is almost complete. A group of incredible writers, including Shane, have helped me create a bunch of songs that I could not be prouder of, and we are choosing which ten to take into the studio and finish up. My manager, Robert Carlton, and I have exhausted ourselves, carefully weighing each song and how it could possibly enrich or take away from the project as a whole.

On the home front, we were finally able to get out of the financial weeds a little bit. We didn't have a hot tub or anything, but I wasn't having trouble sleeping anymore. As I reflected on recent years, I thought a ton about Craig and his family and still couldn't grasp why in the world they were so generous. I just didn't understand it. They had nothing to gain by loving us. But they loved us. I jokingly thanked him often, like I would thank my dad for something, with a punch on the arm. I mean, come on; how do you thank someone for unconditional love . . . and a van. It's impossible.

So, I started processing my feelings the way I always do. Through a song. I sat down at the piano and just started playing and talking. "I met Craig at a church called Redeeming Grace . . ."

"Craig"
Walker Hayes

I met Craig at a church called Redeeming Grace
It's like he understood my "I don't want to be here" face
I felt out of place & I smelled like beer
But he just shook my hand & said, "I'm glad you're here"
He says, "We'll all be judged"
But he was never judgmental
And even though my songs don't belong in no hymnal
He'd quote my lyrics, slap me on the back
Said, "Man, you gotta gift. How you write like that?"

(Chorus)
Yeah, I know, he sounds cool, right?
Not your typical kid from Sunday School, right?
I still ain't figured out church yet
But Craig, I get . . .
Nah, he can't walk on water or turn it Napa Valley red
But he just might be tight with a man that did
Nah, he's not the light of the world
But I wish that mine was bright as his
Yeah, he just might be tight with a man that is.

When you lose a record deal, y'all, the perks fade fast
Dealership said, "We're gonna need to get that minivan back"
So, we were down to one car & broke as I felt
Had my wife & six kids and only five seat belts

I needed help, but couldn't admit I was strugglin'
Said, "Craig, it's all good"
But he knew it all wasn't
A "Hey, man, I'm prayin' for ya" woulda been sufficient
But nah, he took roadside assistance to a whole notha level
To sacrificial heights
Showed up at the ballpark after my son's game one night
In two cars, with his wife, Laura, watching from the other
I said, "What in the world are y'all doing here, brotha?"
He just laughed beside that old Chrysler Town & Country van
With the keys & the title & a pen in his hand said
"Man, all you gotta do is sign & it's y'alls"
I said "Nuh uh, no way"
But he wouldn't take nah for an answer
He said, "Please, dude. Somebody did this for me once,
just let me do this for you"
We argued about it for a little while
Then I teared up, and Craig smiled . . .

(Chorus)

My pride was way too ashamed to be adequately grateful at the moment
But I signed the dotted line & I drove the kids home
And when a cop pulled up beside us at the light they didn't have to duck
Cuz thanks to Craig they were all buckled up . . .[1]

I worked a little on the song in my spare time. Nothing pressing. I just wanted to finish it and give it to Craig. As I got deeper and deeper into the lyric, I have to admit I was like, "This is actually pretty good." I wasn't thinking "radio good," but I thought it was clever. I'm sad to say now, but the thing I found most brilliant about the song was that I did not say the name of Jesus in it, since I didn't believe in Him. The song took me several months to finish. I would just think of lines at random times on random days and add them when I had a chance. I would play what I had come up with for Laney occasionally and make sure all the details were exactly how the story went.

When I was finally happy with what I had, I emailed the song to myself, like I do with all my stuff. I listened to it in my car. It was sick! But I had some serious cold feet now that it was time to send it to Craig. I mean, what dude writes a song for another dude? The more I thought about it, the more I second-guessed playing it for him. Laney said I had to send it, that she thought it would encourage the Coopers, and she promised it wasn't weird at all. I still didn't have the guts, so she finally just emailed it to Laura herself. Later that night, Laney showed me the text from Laura that said something to the effect of, "Craig is speechless."

We were exactly one day away from going into the studio when I turned the song in to my team. I had absolutely no intention of putting it on an album since it was so personal. I had mentioned a lyric or two to Robert, and he had encouraged me to finish, but I never expected the reaction I received from him and Shane. I shared it with Rob first, and he immediately shared it with Shane that afternoon. Shane was blown away. We recorded it with a full band the next day, and it became the last song on my debut album, *boom*.[2]

I remember the musicians in the studio being incredibly moved by the message of the song. That was flattering since those guys have played on some pretty iconic records. Immediately out of the gate, I noticed the song had an incredibly unique impact on people that I had not anticipated. It was a little bit weird to me how a story so specific and personal to my life impacted others so deeply. Even my dad, who was my most brutally honest critic and not a huge hip-hop fan, called me in tears saying it was the best song I'd ever written. He was so emotional, I could barely understand what he was saying. While he was going on and on about it, I could hear someone saying hello to him in the background. He actually hurriedly hung up on me so he could play it for whoever that was!

Months later, I stood as the opening act in front of a sold-out crowd at the Ryman Auditorium. I watched Craig smiling in the audience while I sang the song "Craig." It was surreal to say the least. I would imagine for both of us.

CRAIG

A FEW SUMMERS AGO, our family took a trip to the coast of Maine. We rented a little cottage in Hancock. Splitting the cost between our family and Laura's family, we spent several days in the area surrounding Acadia National Park together. Laura had been to Maine many times, as her family vacationed there often during her childhood, but this was my first time, and it was a first for our kids.

The coast of Maine is unlike anything I have ever seen. The North Atlantic Ocean crashes on jagged, rocky edges, stealing your breath away, and the flora is gorgeous. We took nature hikes in Winter Harbor. We climbed the mountainous peaks of Acadia and dined on inexpensive local lobster tails amidst stunning views of Bar Harbor. We went out on many canoe rides across the channel that connected our backyard to deserted islands, and we boarded boat rides to remote destinations.

One of my favorite moments, though, was when we took the family hiking in a little area called Blue Hill. Made famous by the children's book *Blueberries for Sal,* Blue Hill is the spot that Little Sal and her mother climbed in search of blueberries. Laura had read the book to our kids many times when they were young, so she was able to quote the prose from memory in the van as we approached the iconic spot.

Climbing the hill to the top is a bit of a feat, and it wasn't long before little feet grew tired. Our youngest daughter, Penelope, was ready to turn back. Having just turned seven years old a few days before, she was struggling with the hike. I had just recovered from a serious back injury and wasn't about to put Penelope on my shoulders for the remainder of the trek. So, I stopped to consider our options. The idea came to me to halt the entire group and put Penelope in front, encouraging her that *she* would be the one to lead us to the top of Blue Hill.

Penelope's eyes lit up and she immediately rose to the challenge, excited. Springing into action, she started climbing the hill with the rest of us following behind. Within half an hour, my daughter led us right to the top, where we beheld one of the most glorious views of our entire trip in Maine. Watching Penelope spread her arms open wide with a huge smile on her face welcoming the rest of us to the top of Blue Hill is a moment I'll never forget as a dad.

"We made it!" Penelope said, "and it feels amazing!" Reflecting on this hike, I realized that sometimes God intentionally puts the weakest in the front of the pack. He delights to use the frail to guide the strong. He often chooses the depleted, the ones who've run out of their own energy, to blaze a trail for others in order to make it clear to everyone that *He* is the strength we all need. What matters most is not the order of where we're standing in line on a hike, but the stunning vistas of God's own glory and grace all around us. God arrests our attention with His creation. Penelope didn't create the view we all enjoyed that day, and she certainly wasn't the most qualified to guide us to the top, but as her father, I had selected *her* to lead us all in

> *I see now that God was positioning me in the front of a line of countless others scaling a mountain of grace that would lead to spectacular sceneries of His own handiwork. God takes delights in using the depleted to display the power of His own grace for His joy and ours.*

that moment—for her joy and ours. And what a joyful moment it was!

The night we gave the Hayeses our family van, all I was trying to do was meet a need for a dear friend I loved. Looking back, I see now that God was positioning me, as I had positioned Penelope, in the front of a line of countless others scaling a mountain of grace that would lead to spectacular sceneries of His own handiwork. God takes delights in using the depleted to display the power of His own grace for His joy and ours.

* * *

It was a hot summer night, and Laura and I were out on a date. We had just finished dinner and were sitting in the parking lot of a movie theatre in Franklin, debating whether to even go inside. I had just returned from a weekend ministry trip, and I had been sharing with Laura how deeply discouraged I was. The disappointments of my past had assaulted me like an armed battalion over the course of the weekend. By the time I had driven home, I was feeling like an utter failure in life and in ministry. At this point, we were approaching the fifth anniversary of our little church plant in middle Tennessee, and I was seriously questioning my calling and overall purpose in the world. I had even reached out to the other pastors of our church and shared with the team that I wasn't sure if I should be in ministry any longer. I just couldn't see any fruitfulness coming from my efforts, and I was just so depleted from balancing ministry alongside the demands of a full-time job. Earlier that

> **The disappointments of my past had assaulted me like an armed battalion over the course of the weekend. By the time I had driven home, I was feeling like an utter failure in life and in ministry.**

day, I had taken a long walk in my local town square, praying through my melancholy, head hung low, feet barely shuffling one after the other. I stopped mid-walk and looked up into the sky and said to God: "Father, You know that I try to encourage others, and I'm so discouraged right now. I really need You to encourage *me*. Please, Lord, show me that You're with me. Is *anything* I'm doing here making a difference in *anyone's* life?"

I had been mulling over how I had left a full-time ministry position in east Tennessee, relocated my family to Nashville, and started working a full-time job with a staffing firm in order to help plant a church as a pastor without pay, and I was beginning to wonder if it was worth it all.

I was sharing all of this with Laura, tears in my eyes, as we sat in the car on our date when her phone buzzed with a notification from Laney.

Laura opened the note. Honestly, I was a little peeved that she was checking her phone while I was trying to share the deep recesses of my heart with her, but she quickly said, "There's a file here from Walker, and it's just titled, 'Craig'; I really think we should open it." We were accustomed to receiving files from Walker of songs he was working on, but a file with my name on it? That was a surprise.

"Let's just open that later, Laura," I said sighing. But, she persisted, saying it might help, and then she just connected it to the speakers and played the song, "Craig."

I can't adequately describe the moment I first heard the song. Walker was a professing atheist, an admitted unbeliever. Yes, he had become a very dear friend, but he was the last person I would have thought God would have used in that moment to encourage me; yet that is exactly why it encouraged me so much. Walker was clearly acknowledging the reality of Christ *in my life*, and I sat in the car with my wife and wept as we listened, absolutely stunned.

For years, I have prayed, "God, please use me for your glory; make my life like a finger pointing to Christ." This song was an answer to those prayers. Walker masterfully pointed *my* attention back to Jesus. In such a creative way, he highlighted to me that he understood what matters most in my life is my relationship with Jesus, and that my relationship with Jesus is what inspired me to give him our van. It was the strongest form of encouragement I could receive, and he did it all without even saying the name of Jesus.

In an incredible demonstration of God's sovereign goodness, power, and love, the Lord had encouraged me through my unbelieving friend that He indeed had me right where He wanted me, that He was still with me, that He *was* hearing my prayers, and that He *was* using my life to make a difference for His glory—at least with my friend Walker. With the words of the song "Craig" rising through the stereo of our car, I was reminded of, and arrested by, the truths of Zephaniah 3:17:

> The LORD your God is in your midst,
>> a mighty one who will save;
> he will rejoice over you with gladness;
>> he will quiet you by his love;
> he will exult over you with loud singing.

I strangely sensed the Lord Himself singing over me through Walker's voice, and I was undone. I couldn't even respond, so I asked Laura to respond for me:

"Speechless."

I had no other words.

Even as I write this, I'm overwhelmed with emotion as if that moment were just yesterday.

I had come to know Walker well, well enough to know that something strangely supernatural was taking place when he sent us the song "Craig." I was reminded how on several occasions I had asked God to use Walker's gifts of songwriting to draw others' attention to Jesus, though Walker himself was not a follower of Christ. I was reminded how I had prayed regularly that the Lord would draw Walker to Himself, even through his own songs. This was way more than a thank-you note from Walker to our family for giving his family a van. It was the first inkling to me that the Lord was answering prayers and doing something supernatural in my friend's life, something that could only be attributed to God Himself.

The song "Craig" was never intended for anyone's ears but mine and Laura's, and that's the way I wanted it. We kept the song so tight to our chests that we didn't even play it for our own kids until one day after they heard about it from Walker himself and started asking us why we had not yet played it for them. I finally gathered our crew upstairs and shared with them how meaningful the song was to us, how we saw it as an answer to my prayers for encouragement from the Lord, how we were continuing to pray for Walker to become a Christian, and how we didn't want the kids sharing about the song with anyone else. We told them it was a private expression of thanks from Walker, and we wanted our family to keep it that way. I asked the kids to commit to not talking about it with anyone before I would play it for them. They all agreed, and we all sat in wonder in our upstairs living room as I played them the song. Then we prayed for Walker and thanked God for the work He was doing in our friend.

It was perplexing to us when Walker called many days later saying that his producer loved the song and wanted it added as the final track of his first album with Monument Records. Our family had worked hard to keep the giving of the van a secret, and we had kept the song a secret, but it was becoming clear that God had different plans.

Maybe you wonder, like I did, if your life is making *any* difference in the world around you—any positive impact on others' lives. Maybe you're struggling to find meaning in the midst of all the mundane, everyday stuff of your ordinary life. I can relate. If that's you, please let this story encourage you. You may not see it now, but your life *is* making a difference to the world around you. And more importantly, God is rejoicing over you. I think a lot of people, even heartfelt believers in Christ, don't truly feel loved or accepted by God. We can often picture God as a disinterested father, cross with us, mildly irritated, maybe even rolling His eyes in our direction. If we don't see Him as agitated, we can think of Him as merely tolerating us, but certainly not rejoicing over us. How could He, with all the baggage we bring? Yet the Bible portrays God as *singing over us* with gladness (Zeph. 3:17). There's no compulsion there. It is His joy. Scripture says that God will quiet us with His love, and He will exult over us with singing.

> **You may not see it now, but your life is making a difference to the world around you. And more importantly, God is rejoicing over you.**

The truth is, you and I can be much more aware of our own faults and failures than we are of the faithfulness of God and His expressed feelings of delight in us. That's why we need a biblical view of Jesus, one where He already knows everything about us and yet He still rejoices in us. That's the true heart of Christ.

I love the way Dane Ortlund communicates this in his book *Gentle and Lowly.* Dane writes,

Jesus is not trigger-happy. Not harsh, reactionary, easily exasperated. He is the most understanding person in the universe. The posture most natural to him is not a pointed finger but open arms. . . . No one in human history has ever been more approachable than Jesus Christ. No prerequisites. No hoops to jump through. . . . The minimum bar to be enfolded into the embrace of Jesus is simply: open yourself up to him. It is all he needs. Indeed, it is the only thing he works with.[3]

The posture of Jesus is one of open arms. Warmth. Empathy. Welcome. Joy. Jesus' love is a love that sings over us with rejoicing. Dear believer, that's God's heart for you. You don't have to be perfect to be used by God. You don't have to walk on water or be able to turn it Napa Valley red—if you know and are known by the One who did; if you draw near to Him and simply open yourself up to receive and reflect His love, there's no telling what God can do in and through you. He may even stop the hike you're on to put you in the front of the pack in order to display His glory through your lack of strength. Regardless, He delights in you and wants you to feel and know His great love.

WALKER'S INSTAGRAM POST, MAY 23, 2018

I felt a responsibility as an artist to put "Craig" out as my second single. I know it's not the easiest option for country radio to play. I know it takes a listen or two for people to embrace the message. I know it's alarmingly different and stylistically polarizing. But it's the truth, and every time I sing it, I mean it . . . I feel it . . . and I know it means something to someone listening. . . .

The reactions to "Craig" have spoken. I've met countless people who are reminded of the "Craigs" in their lives. I've met countless people who are inspired to be like Craig. I've met countless people who have been inspired by the song to give cards to families in need, pay it forward, adopt children, etc. in response to the song. It's crazy what the story of Craig and me is causing . . . And as an artist, that's what it's all about . . . Telling the world about things that change us . . . That's why I had to put this song out.

Craig and his family and their example mean everything to me. I needed them. I must tell y'all about em. I want to introduce them to everyone.[4]

8

BABY

WALKER

I call Shane my Sh-angel because from the moment I started working with him, my career had new life. It most definitely didn't happen overnight; but looking back, it seems like he snapped, and I had a top ten record. My first single, "You Broke Up With Me," flew up the country charts and hung at number nine for about a month! Then it died. But it was a wild ride, and my schedule was slammed. I spent about a year traveling the country and visiting radio stations everywhere, trying to sell them on my music. I was on morning shows, opening for some pretty massive artists, and our trajectory was like a rocket!

Laney seemed happy. She was pregnant with our seventh baby at home. I think she was appreciative of the financial stability the success provided. After so many years wondering if we were going to make it another month, it was awful nice to hear from our financial team that we wouldn't run out of money for a year or two. Laney and I would laugh and say, "We're rich!" It was so nice to feel relief in that department. Our kids were doing well, minus the fact that I was always gone. I would make it to as many games and events as I could, but it wasn't enough. Laney was so sweet during those times too. She would repeatedly assure me she could handle the kids and life with me being away all the time just fine. She would say she just missed my company. This always broke my heart but made me feel like I was doing the right thing: working while I had the work.

However, success let me down early, as work became an addiction. Nothing was enough. I said yes to every show on the table. I watched the charts and my socials religiously. No matter what was going on, I needed more. I remember when "You Broke Up With Me" went platinum, the first thoughts in my head as I held the plaque were, "Man, I have to do this again?" and "Dang, this doesn't feel as good as I thought it would." Everyone around me was celebrating while I sat in the shadows of the future, wondering how in the world I could maintain this pace. I was exhausted.

> **Everyone around me was celebrating, while I sat in the shadows of the future, wondering how in the world I could maintain this pace. I was exhausted.**

In the summer of 2018, life was at its busiest. I had scheduled a couple weeks home aiming for the birth of our seventh child. I was home for the last ultrasound about five days before the due date, and the technician told us everything was perfect.

On June 6th, Laney went into labor. It was about six in the morning. She acted like she felt fine, and her contractions were speeding up. We had agreed together to do a home birth. We'd had some pretty close calls in the past, barely making it to the hospital in time. Beckett was almost born on I-65! I remember getting the van up to 115 mph on that trip. We didn't want to do that again, and Laney had thoroughly researched our options. We both agreed a home birth was for us.

The timing was pretty complicated. I didn't really know how the next few days would pan out. I was supposed to sing on national television on the CMT awards that night. It would be my first award show performance appearance. Massive exposure. Then I was supposed to hop on a bus that night to a weekend's worth of shows. I was thinking it wouldn't be ideal, but it would work to meet the baby, hop over and crush the awards show, then go back to the hospital and be with Laney and the baby till I had to get on the bus. Recalling that I was actually going to prioritize work over my wife like that makes me nauseous. To think that I would have left my wife and newborn child so easily makes me wanna go back to that version of me and punch him in the face.

Laney's midwife arrived and began to walk her through some contractions. I was frantically running around trying to help but really doing nothing. Laney's threshold for pain is through the roof. A silent Laney is indicative of pain. She doesn't scream at me or moan in pain when she has a baby. She just doesn't say anything. It's quite confusing at times, since I am someone who appreciates an overdose of communication. It's been a lifelong joke between us.

At some point, the midwife asked me to get Laney a Gatorade. Just one of those things I won't ever forget. There was a moment where I began to wonder if something was off about this labor. Laney wasn't just quiet; she seemed like she was in more pain than usual. She was on our bed and her eyes were looking glazed. Her face looked more exhausted than I'd ever seen it in labor. Honestly, I was used to these things happening so fast and effortlessly. I know that probably sounds insensitive, but she had just made it look so easy in the past. This one was different. When I got back to the bedroom with a Gatorade I had snagged from our next-door neighbor, the midwife was checking the baby's heartbeat. When I left to get the Gatorade, the heartbeat was strong. When I returned after a few minutes, the midwife said she couldn't find it. She suggested we call 911.

When the EMTs arrived, they quickly checked Laney's vitals and got her into the ambulance. The lights from the ambulance had attracted a few neighbors out to the sidewalks of our street. Our kids were still asleep upstairs, and I remember asking a neighbor if she minded camping out at our house so someone would be there when they woke up.

The ambulance sped us through downtown Franklin to Williamson Medical Center, our closest hospital. Laney's eyes were open, but I could tell she had no idea what was going on. I'd never seen her like this in my life. It's like she was stuck somewhere between passing out and waking up. I was not allowed to ride in the back with her and watched traffic not get out of the way as we drove there.

I've never been that scared. I wanted to help her, but I had no idea how. Arriving at the hospital was a blur. Laney was rushed to a room where a doctor hastily assessed the situation while what seemed like a billion nurses attached tubes and machines to her. The chaos went from sixty to zero in about two seconds when they took her to an operating room. I tried to follow but I wasn't allowed to go any further.

I paced back and forth in the room. Assuming all the worst possible outcomes and then trying to talk my head out of believing they could happen. I could hear the clock above the door ticking. I wondered whether our baby was a boy or girl and if they were ok. I wondered if Laney was dying. I wondered what was going on inside of her. I wondered what our last conversation was and how it had ended.

After the longest fifteen minutes of my life, the doctor knocked and took a couple steps inside the room. She informed me that our baby was a girl. She told me that they tried to resuscitate but she didn't make it. My body still remembers how that felt. I can feel it now as I'm typing. I was destroyed. I had failed at protecting my daughter. She died. Right as she was beginning her life, she died. I was right there as her heart stopped, and I couldn't make it not stop. The only thing between me and her was the skin of Laney's tummy, and I let her die. She was almost to us.

The doctor proceeded to tell me that Laney had suffered a serious uterine rupture and was still bleeding and that their focus now was making it stop. So, my mind went from the loss of our little girl to Laney's life. The door shut and I crumbled. I've never felt that alone. I contemplated busting through the hospital just to touch Laney's hand once. I justified that it would be worth getting arrested if it was the last time we held hands. I contemplated begging the doctor to try to resuscitate our daughter again, as if it would make a difference. I thought about some crazy stuff.

The doctor kept coming back and bringing me up to speed on what was happening. She was very professional and kind. About every fifteen minutes or so she would tell me that they were doing everything they could to slow and stop the bleeding and that Laney was receiving massive blood transfusions. This happened about three or four times until she finally came in and said it had stopped. She confessed that she didn't know how it had stopped. She explained the science of it to me and why it didn't make sense that it had stopped, but it had stopped. I wasn't really in a place where I could absorb information, but I was just so grateful my best friend was alive. When the doctor left, and the door was shut, I fell to my knees and cried. Hours later someone came in and escorted me to the intensive care waiting room where I was seated until I could go in and see Laney.

Craig was in the waiting room. I gave him a few-sentences-long version of what had happened, and we wept. Man to man. He held me in his arms while I hurt. I couldn't talk. When I was able to say a word or two, I asked if he minded bringing my oldest daughter, Lela, to the hospital. I needed her there with me. She is Laney's mini-me. She's my buddy. I hadn't spoken with the kids and told them what had happened yet. I know that had to have been painful for Craig. Driving a twelve-year-old little girl to the hospital who thinks she's coming to meet her newborn sister, while knowing the terrible news she was about to receive.

In the meantime, I was allowed to go back and see Laney. She was waking up slowly. She looked dead. Her body was freezing. She had a tube down her throat and was very, very groggy. I was devastated just seeing her like that. When she woke up enough to move, she looked into my eyes and patted her belly. I could tell she wanted to know what happened to our baby. This was the worst part. Choking up, I explained that it was a girl and that she didn't make it. As I watched her face process the news, tears began rolling from her eyes. Her body convulsed. She cried herself to sleep for a few minutes and then woke up again. When she looked at me this time, I could tell she didn't remember anything I'd said before. She tapped her belly once more, wondering what had happened, and I broke her heart again with the news. This continued for about an hour until she was finally awake, and I saw a sadness fall over Laney like I'd never seen. Laney has always been full of life. She is synonymous with a smile. I've never felt more helpless than I did with her that day. Seeing such a vibrant soul crushed like that and not being able to undo it just about killed me.

I will never forget sitting beside her as she was coming to, writing each other notes back and forth on a small white board, since she still had a tube down her throat. She couldn't write that well because her body was still waking up and she had wires and IVs attached but she managed to write, "Can't do this again. Adopt." I nodded my head in agreement, and we cried together.

When they took the tube out of Laney's mouth and she was completely coherent, they brought our baby in. Oakleigh Klover Hayes. She was beautiful. She had a head full of dark hair. She had a tiny scratch near her eye where something had obviously nicked her during emergency surgery. Everything about her was perfect except she was dead. She felt cold. It was weird, wanting to warm her in a nurturing way, knowing she wasn't alive. It was heart crushing to watch Laney cradle and kiss her lifeless daughter. We looked at her hands and feet and fingers and toes. We compared her characteristics to our others when they were newborn. We hurt.

When Craig showed up with Lela, I walked with her about halfway down the hall towards Laney's room and stopped. I tried to speak, but words wouldn't come out. Somehow, I eventually articulated what had happened, that it was a girl, and that she didn't make it, and that mom looked pretty rough but was on her way back to normal. My young daughter actually consoled me in the hall as I broke the news and then we entered Laney's room. Lela is such a special person to us. She has been not only a daughter but such a merciful, forgiving companion in our lives. She has seen all versions of us and has so graciously helped us learn how to be parents. On that day, she truly carried me down that hall. I was so thankful to have her strength beside me.

I was able to bring Craig and Laura back. We all snuggled Oakleigh. We passed her around and talked about how beautiful she was. We cried and cried and cried some more. It just hurt. I can't explain it. The pain. Holding her. Watching Laney hold her. Watching Craig and Laura and Lela hold her. I just wished so bad she would wake up. So bad. I just stared at her eyes hoping they would open. That her fingers would move. That her ribs would breathe in and out. But they didn't.

To have these memories of Craig and Laura holding our daughter. To know someone is hurting with us on the exact same level—just, wow. Remembering their faces as they held her breaks my heart in the best way. That is Christ.

I drove home that day to tell the kids what had happened. I can't remember who all was in our house, but I asked them to give us a minute while I spoke with the kids. I sat them on the couch and got on my knees and told them the whole story. They all took it differently. I did my best to answer each of their questions and console them. They were blindsided. Our little girls were too young to really embrace what had happened, but the rest were pretty upset. I feel sorry for our kids because Laney would have known better how to appropriately break the news to them. I did the best I could. I remember sitting at a red light on the way back to the hospital looking around at everyone else in traffic thinking how weird it was that my world had stopped while theirs just continued.

We kept Oakleigh with us for the rest of the day. What a hopeless feeling when they took her away. It was just so final. She wasn't coming back. Laney and I were confused. We were torn apart. Laney's body was physically torn apart. We decided there would be no easy time to let her go and the longer we held her the harder it would be to say goodbye. So, we let them take her that night.

Laney's body healed well over the next few days. It was so odd being in the hospital and going through all the similar, yet extreme, procedures of having a baby with nothing to show for it. All those months Laney carried this child inside her and then we left the hospital, just us. No baby in the back seat. We were immediately pressed with the task and business of burial when we got home. We had to figure out a cemetery and a service and all the details that went along with losing a child. Cremation was an option, but we just couldn't do it to her little body. I know that was just her shell. She wasn't really there, but we couldn't.

As soon as we could, we visited a cemetery recommended to us by a family that had also had a stillborn. It was depressing. There was nowhere beautiful enough to bury our little girl. Every plot, every space paled in comparison to her. However, we did settle on a spot that felt right. We were wandering around and actually came across the gravesite of the little girl from the family that had told us about this particular cemetery. Her name was Lucy. While we stood there hurting for her family and ourselves, a dog walked out from the nearby woods and joined us. He kind of hung with us for a sec, then trotted over to a random gravestone. When he lifted his leg and peed on it, Laney and I laughed out loud for the second time since we lost Oakleigh. We knew it was the perfect place for her. There were dogs peeing everywhere and kids everywhere, just like our home. The first time we laughed after losing Oakleigh was on our first visit to the cemetery when the man helping us introduced himself. He said, "I'm Barry." I snickered, "What are the odds? A guy named Barry who works at a cemetery and buries people." That made us chuckle a little bit.

We buried Oakleigh on a Friday. I was mad and Laney was sad. That's how we grieve. I could immediately see how couples rarely make it through the loss of a child. It sends you both spiraling in opposite directions. We showed up at the cemetery early and gathered around Oakleigh one last time. This nice lady that worked there, caring for Oakleigh's body, showed our kids a cute little teddy bear that she put in the casket. She gave us an identical bear for the kids to keep. It was sweet. I wouldn't want her job. Our kids drew pictures and wrote letters to put in the casket. Chapel (ten at the time) made her a lego heart and included his most rare Pokemon card.

We rode over to the gravesite with our kiddos, and Craig and Laura were there. There were some chairs for us to sit in and Craig spoke. Honestly, I suggested Craig speak, for Laney's sake. I was most definitely not buying the whole Jesus thing, especially at this moment in my life, but I wouldn't deny Laney a Christian burial for our baby. Honestly, y'all, we were just going through the motions at this point. Doing a lot of what people suggested because we hadn't experienced anything like this before.

> *I was mad and Laney was sad. That's how we grieve. I could immediately see how couples rarely make it through the loss of a child. It sends you both spiraling in opposite directions.*

Oakleigh's initials were O.K. Craig talked about how she was "O.K." in heaven. This kind of frustrated me, but I understood the softball it lobbed to Craig for an out-of-the-park funeral speech. I wasn't O.K.

Regardless of my attitude at the time, Craig spoke beautifully to the sound of us sniffling. At one point, I knelt and just bear-hugged the casket with all my strength. I think Laney fell with me on her knees. We were a mess. It was so hot outside. I remember sweating like crazy. My sons, Chapel, Baylor, and Beckett, helped me carry her casket to the graveside and after they lowered it into the hole, we filled it up with dirt together. I'm grateful the cemetery let us do that. That was healing.

While we were overwhelmed with pain, we were also overwhelmed with gratitude. Shane and Michael McAnally Baum paid for Oakleigh's burial. Every dime of it. Food and groceries were taken care of for the next three months. Even people we'd never met pitched in.

Of course, Craig and Laura were also by our sides with us in this storm. The mess was messy. For me, the hope was invisible. Laney was inconsolable. I was furious. Nothing about us was inviting. It would have been easy to say regarding us, "I don't know what to say so I will just not say anything and just give them space." But Craig and Laura were present. And somehow, wherever the grace was coming from inside them was relentless. They fearlessly got all up in the awkwardness of real pain and waded through it with us. They were family.

Laney and the kids and I drove home in silence. That afternoon, I felt self-destructive. I had so much anger and nothing to do with it. I just wanted to fight. So, I got in my car and drove into downtown Franklin. I hadn't had a drink in two years, but I decided I deserved it. During the three-mile drive I planned what I was going to do. I was going to go to a bar and drink rapidly. I was going to pick a large man, preferably with some other dudes, and provoke them until it went down. Then I was just going to fight till I couldn't. I figured I'd surely be arrested. But I would go hard until then. I had it all planned out. When I parked in front of the bar, I reached into the pocket of my driver's side door and realized my wallet wasn't there. I couldn't find it, so I turned around and drove home to get it.

When I walked in the front door of our house, I saw Laney on the couch by herself and it hit me, I'm a terrible husband. There my wife was. Still physically wounded from birthing a dead baby. Mentally struggling with the loss of her child and the loss of being able to have the future kids we dreamed of. And there I was selfishly deciding I deserved to check out. Selfishly abandoning my entire family and almost dumping more mess on top of the mess. The last thing they needed amidst the anguish they were already feeling was to bail their husband and dad out of jail. Not to mention the falling-off-the-wagon part. I broke down and confessed to Laney what I had almost done. It was a low moment. I was apologetic, and she was merciful. She googled and found a random AA meeting to attend. That was the only thing we could think of.

On my way to the meeting that night I saw both ends of a giant rainbow over Highway 96. It was perfect. I'll never forget it. I parked and walked past some folks smoking outside the meeting. I walked inside and didn't say a word to anyone. I poured a Styrofoam cup of coffee, picked a plastic folding chair out of the circle, and sat down. I avoided all eye contact and just stared at the dirt still on my shoes from the graveside. I kid you not. The first guy that stood up to tell his story that night began his spiel with the words, "I was angry . . ." I could relate.

I left the meeting that night without a word. I'm sad to say I didn't even take the chance to tell that guy how much his words meant to me at a time when nothing meant anything to me. I called Craig and poured it all out. Craig listened and said he'd had a restless afternoon as well.

I told him what I'd almost done and just hurt out loud. He hurt too.

CRAIG

AT THIS POINT, the Hayeses felt like an extension of our family. Walker and I were best of friends, and Laura and Laney felt closer than sisters. Our dogs *were* sisters from the same litter, and our kids were all close friends. Walker was on the road a lot, so we spent as much time together as we could when he was home, typically celebrating birthdays and major events together. We were all looking forward to baby Oakleigh's arrival.

On June 6, 2018, I had just left an early morning work event, and I was driving south from Nashville to Franklin on I-65 when I received the call from my wife. I knew Laney was in labor at home with a midwife, and I was expecting the good news about the arrival of Oakleigh. Instead, Laura was crying uncontrollably.

"Craig, Walker needs you at the hospital . . . Oakleigh didn't make it . . . Laney's in intensive care, and I'm heading to their house to take care of the kids. Please pray. And please go to the hospital with Walker."

I was shaking by the time I arrived at Williamson Medical. Eyes blurred, I walked into the room where Walker sat stunned and speechless.

I hugged him hard.

We wept together.

In a moment, doctors came in and out of the room with updates, and we learned that Laney's uterus had ruptured during labor. She had lost so much blood that it was a mercy that she was still alive, but Oakleigh didn't survive.

There are no words for a moment like this. Only tears.

Walker wanted Lela there, his oldest daughter. I told him I would pick her up. So, I left the hospital and drove to the Hayeses home to retrieve Lela, while Laura stayed in their home with the kids.

The Hayes kids didn't know Oakleigh had died, and they didn't know the severity of the situation their mom was in, so it was a challenging ride from their home to the hospital as Lela peppered me with questions about how her mom was doing and who little Oakleigh looked like most in the family. I wanted so badly just to hug Lela and weep, but I also wanted her dad to be the one to tell her, so I inwardly asked God to please strengthen me as we drove.

When I escorted Lela to Walker, he shared the news with her. I've never felt pain quite like that moment. We grieved for Oakleigh, and we prayed for Laney.

Several hours later, we learned that Laney's condition was stable and she was conscious. Laney asked for me and Laura to come in and see little Oakleigh. I entered the hospital room, hugged Laney, kissed her on the forehead, and said, "You scared us so much; I'm so glad you're okay, and I'm so sorry about Oakleigh." I was just heartbroken. Oakleigh was gorgeous, absolutely beautiful, and perfect in every way, yet there was no breath or life in her body. Laney asked if we would like to hold her. We took turns embracing little Oakleigh, her stunning form lying peacefully still in our arms.

> *I can still feel the weight of her body whenever I gaze at the pictures the photographer took in those quiet and heavy moments of unspeakable grief.*

We stayed in the room for a long time weeping together.

I can still feel the weight of her body whenever I gaze at the pictures the photographer took in those quiet and heavy moments of unspeakable grief.

* * *

Several years prior, Walker and I participated together in a funeral for a child and his mother who passed away after a terrible car accident. The boy was a teammate on one of my son's sports teams. The father had lost his wife and his son on the same day, and he asked if I would officiate the funeral, as I was the only pastor he knew. Walker and I had run the scoreboard together on numerous occasions, so we both knew the boy and his father. When I was asked to officiate the funeral, I asked Walker if he would be willing to play a few songs. It was a heart-wrenching experience for both of us. Neither of us could have ever imagined that we would one day be in the position where we were attending a funeral together for one of our own children.

In the days to come, Walker and Laney picked out a burial plot in Nashville. They asked if I would officiate Oakleigh's funeral. Walker and Laney wanted a small service with just me and Laura and their family.

I've attended and officiated many funerals, but the day we buried Oakleigh Klover Hayes was one of the hardest days of my life.

I read from the prophet Isaiah:

And [the LORD of hosts] will swallow up on this mountain
the covering that is cast over all peoples,
the veil that is spread over all nations.
He will swallow up death forever;
and the Lord GOD will wipe away tears from all faces,
and the reproach of his people he will take away from all the earth,
for the LORD has spoken.
It will be said on that day,
"Behold, this is our God; we have waited for him, that he might save us.
This is the LORD; we have waited for him;
let us be glad and rejoice in his salvation." (25:7–9)

And then from Luke,

Now they were bringing even infants to [Jesus] that he might touch them. And when the disciples saw it, they rebuked them. But Jesus called them to him, saying, *"Let the children come to me, and do not hinder them, for to such belongs the kingdom of God. Truly, I say to you, whoever does not* receive the kingdom of God like a child shall not enter it." (18:15–17)

I shared for a moment about how Jesus embraces infants and little children and how He said that to such belongs the kingdom of God.

I shared how infants can't do anything but receive, and that heaven belongs to those who simply receive the mercy and kindness of God in Christ for their salvation.

I told of great people of God throughout the centuries whose infants had died, including the psalmist David and how in 2 Samuel, when David learned that his child had died, the text reads,

> Then David arose from the earth and washed and anointed himself and changed his clothes. And he went into the house of the LORD and worshiped. He then went to his own house. And when he asked, they set food before him, and he ate. Then his servants said to him, "What is this thing that you have done? You fasted and wept for the child while he was alive; but when the child died, you arose and ate food." He said, "While the child was still alive, I fasted and wept, for I said, 'Who knows whether the LORD will be gracious to me, that the child may live?' But now he is dead. Why should I fast? Can I bring him back again? *I shall go to him, but he will not return to me.*" (12:20–23).

I was struck by how King David was absolutely convinced that his child would be in heaven, and that David would one day go there to meet him. And I was absolutely convinced that Jesus had little Oakleigh in His care, and that whether we go to heaven as an infant or as an adult, the only way is through Jesus.

I shared how much I loved Oakleigh's name: Oakleigh Klover Hayes. That her initials are O.K., and that she is okay because she's with Jesus. That though we all grieve, we can grieve with hope that though Oakleigh's death is a loss for *us*, it is gain *for her*. Then, I commended to the Almighty God this dear child, Oakleigh Klover Hayes, even as we committed her body to the ground: earth to earth, ashes to ashes, dust to dust.

We prayed, and then Laura and I stepped back as we witnessed Walker and his sons take shovels to the dirt to fill in little Oakleigh's grave.

Absolutely crushed in spirit, I watched it all in bewilderment. Unspeakable suffering. Immeasurable grief.

I was struggling hard that night. I thought if I was struggling, surely Walker was struggling even more than me. So, I called to check on him. He didn't answer, but he later called me back. By this point, Walker had been sober for years, but he told me that he had left his house to drive to a bar with the intent on getting drunk that night. Once he arrived, though, he realized he didn't have his wallet with him, so he returned home, told Laney what had happened, and they found an AA meeting for him to attend within the hour. He had forgotten his wallet, and I was amazed at how God was caring for him even in the midst of all the pain.

* * *

I've had a front-row seat to some pretty amazing redemption stories in my lifetime. Like the day I played piano at my parents' wedding. My mom walked several feet down the "aisle" of our living room as my fingers tickled the ivory of my grandparents' piano to the tune of "Here Comes the Bride." My parents were being reunited after a difficult divorce. I was just a child at the time, about ten years old, so it took several years for me to understand how rare it is that a couple divorced would remarry each other, but I do think that moment marked me as a kid with a strong impression that what has been broken can be restored.

When I look at that restored piano, it sings to me of hope.

That same piano was one of the only things surviving a tornado that leveled my parents' home when I was in college. My dad and mom graciously gifted it to me, and it now sits in the living room of our home. The piano was severely damaged in the storm, so we had to entrust it to an expert in Nashville for restoration. Now, all eighty-eight keys function properly. Many times, as my daughter has played the famous "Clair de Lune" or "Liz On Top of the World" from *Pride and Prejudice*, I'm stopped in my tracks with the thought of how beautiful music can come from broken instruments that have been through tragedy.

When I look at that restored piano, it sings to me of hope. Walker has played that piano on numerous occasions as our families have enjoyed unhurried time together, and my soul lights up every time the melody rises from those keys. I wondered how God could restore the brokenness in my friend Walker's life. I believed He could.

A FRIEND

WALKER

About two weeks after we buried Oakleigh, Laney suggested we return to church. I wasn't really on board, but I was really trying to help her. I can't explain how hard it was to watch Laney hurt. I'd never seen her like this. I'd never seen her so devastated that I couldn't bring her out of it. I couldn't fix her. I couldn't fix myself. But not being able to help your favorite person on this earth sucks. It was so depressing. I knew she wanted to return to Redeeming Grace, so I agreed to support her. Services had moved from Saturday nights to Sunday mornings in a new building since we'd first started going there.

We showed up late like we always do, and a greeter in the back kindly escorted us to the second row on the right side of the church. We were typically left side, back row people. I feel like at church, you just kinda fall into a seating rhythm like you do at your high school cafeteria. You rarely wander from your go-to spot. I remember noticing how different it felt up front. I regretted coming the second we walked in. I still didn't love the place, and since losing Oakleigh, I really just hated everything and everyone.

I'm sure we walked in during the worship part of the service, and I'm sure I was really just glad to sit down when the music was finally over. I was preparing to zone out when I noticed the commotion of people lining up against the wall on our side of the sanctuary. When I saw that it was a bunch of couples holding babies, it hit me. "You gotta be kidding me." Today was baby dedication day. I couldn't believe it, but then again, I could. Church, man. Before I could even think to grab Laney and exit the building, we were sitting face to face with a small parade of families holding their living newborns. The service continued, and Laney lost it. It was an awkward feeling, sitting there trapped in the formality of such a joyful ceremony, but wanting to fight everyone in the room. I know the couples up there felt it too. It's a little church. I've even talked to the pastor since, and he admits he had that "oh, no" feeling when he saw what was about to happen. It was the worst. Laney was obliterated. I could feel her shoulders shaking. I could feel Craig and Laura cringing with us. I was livid. I never wanted to walk in that building again.

Life went on. A few weeks later, we were back at the baseball fields with our kids, learning how to navigate the awkward conversations and condolences you tire of hearing. It's a lose-lose situation. If they say something, it's never the right thing, and if they don't say something, you're mad they didn't mention it. Laney's smiles began to appear more frequently. They looked more and more real as each week passed. However, she refused to hold a baby. It just brought back too many emotions. That was devastating for me to watch the most naturally nurturing person I'd ever known refuse to hold an infant. I tried to get back to work but my job just felt stupid. Life felt pointless. Creative energy was hard to come by, and I had to treat my career like a 9-to-5. Just feed the kids.

I eventually got back on the road but struggled for purpose. Laney and I struggled with our different grieving methods. She appreciated trinkets and cards from certain people, while the same expressions infuriated me and distanced me from them and her. The shrapnel from the explosion woke up a lot of our insecurities and demons that had been at bay for a while. I guess trauma does that to you. Sends you backwards. A lot of our fights reminded me of us as teenagers.

Our different beliefs didn't do us any favors. I remember having to pick out words for Oakleigh's tombstone and thinking all of Laney's suggestions were terrible. I eventually settled for a C. S. Lewis quote, "I was made for another world," to just get her off the subject.

One afternoon, Laney and I were in the backyard purging, throwing away as much stuff as we could. This older man driving by began to slow down. I was pushing an old refrigerator to the curb, hoping he would just keep driving, but he stopped and climbed out of his car. He approached Laney first and started talking. I figured he was just giving her an ear full of the same old "I'm-sorry-for-your-loss" stuff, but I was wrong. Laney got my attention, dragged me into the conversation, and introduced me to Joe. I was annoyed at first, but I gave him my full attention when he explained how he had lost his thirty-year-old son. It was touching. His story shed so much light on the darkness we were experiencing. He quoted a lyric from the song, "It Is Well," and said it was just like the line says, "When sorrows like sea billows roll."[1] He said the waves will continue to come, but they will get further apart in time. He told us they will be unpredictable. Joe was right. That's exactly how moving on is.

The road was tough. Metaphorically and literally speaking. I tried to make my career about the effect it had on others. I tried to motivate myself by making it about the fans and not myself. Those attempts always fired me up for a second, but the fulfillment never lasted. I dove into fitness and working out. I justified my addiction to it by reminding Laney it was healthier than drinking. I came to realize that most of my identity was wrapped up in things I "used." My existence could be narrowed down to my daily list of coping mechanisms. That's all I did in life. Cope. The music was just a never-ending hunt for applause. The gym was just a never-ending search for some unattainable body or strength. Nothing was ever enough. I tried being a better person, but that always lasted about zero minutes. And even if it did last, it came from an impure motive, and I knew it wasn't truly good. I felt gross, but I couldn't get clean.

When I'm out touring, after shows, Laney and I talk on the phone for hours about anything and everything. Every night, I look forward to getting in my bunk and calling her. She's a great listener. She's always understood me from the get-go. Even in high school, at my most misunderstood, she got me. After we lost Oakleigh, something died inside of me, and I don't think it was a bad thing. The things of this world began to grow strangely dim, as one of my favorite hymns says. I began to admit to Laney that I craved transformation. I craved rest.

One time on the road, I met a lady in the meet-and-greet line who had the exact same story as ours. She had six kids, lost her seventh, and her husband was an alcoholic. Unfortunately, he had not recovered yet. As she was saying her goodbyes, she turned to me and said, "I just wish I had a suitcase full of rest to give you." Exactly what I needed! I actually got choked up a little bit thanking her for her wish.

There was one night Laney and I were talking about transformation. I said, "Name one person that has actually been transformed by the gospel." We went back and forth, her naming people and me saying, "Nah, that doesn't count." A lot of the folks she named have most definitely been transformed, but that night I couldn't be convinced. My experience with "Christianity" was a lot of believing something but doing something else. Hypocrisy was synonymous with Christianity in my mind. Regardless, at this point in my life, I was over myself and really wanted freedom from my own hypocrisy, but I just didn't believe Jesus could do what felt like a miracle.

Laney had recently been to this women's group they do at Redeeming Grace called Flourish. I always joked with her about it like, "You gonna 'flourish' tonight?" It sounded so flower-ish. Anyway, she had recently "Flourished," and someone recommended to her a book by a woman named Rosaria Butterfield called, *The Secret Thoughts of an Unlikely Convert*.[2] I pretended I wasn't interested, but in that lonely bus bunk, dying for the cure to life, I was. Laney said she would order me a copy, but when we got off the call, I downloaded it on my phone.

Y'all, this is insane. I am not an avid reader. I go in phases, but I devoured this book. I recommend if anyone is interested in reading an honest look into the transforming power of Jesus, give that book a read. I was challenged. My interest piqued. Rosaria's story and my depravity had a head-on collision. Without spoiling her story, let's just say I could really relate to her pride, and I wanted whatever she

> *I pretended I wasn't interested, but in that lonely bus bunk, dying for the cure to life, I was.*

had. She also had a friend like Craig in her story, and that blew me away.

After reading Rosaria's book, I got home on a Sunday and secretly went to Barnes & Noble and bought a Bible. I kept my head down and hidden as possible, making sure no one in there recognized me. The Bible lived inside the Barnes & Noble bag for several days, so Laney and the kids wouldn't know. I eventually showed them and confessed that I was hungry to learn. That was some ginormous pride to swallow after so many years trying to convince Laney that God was like the Easter bunny. I told Laney how much Rosaria's book had meant to me and we talked about it. I read the Bible every free second I had. I began to meet Jesus, and I'm still meeting Him today.

I told Craig and Laura that I believed in Jesus, or something like that, at a Japanese restaurant in Franklin, and his reaction was priceless. Craig was grateful to God. The tears in his eyes said it all. He even had to retreat to the bathroom for a minute. No doubt he was giving glory to God in the bathroom of Miso! When he hugged me, I'm pretty sure he broke a couple of my ribs. Laura was emotional too. They're so sweet.

God, thank You. Thank You for giving me the desire to know You. Thank You for sending Your Son to rescue me from me. Lord, I pray in Your Son's name that someone buys a Bible after they finish this book. That would be nuts.

CRAIG

C. S. LEWIS HAS FAMOUSLY WRITTEN in *The Problem of Pain* that "God whispers to us in our pleasures, speaks in our conscience, but shouts in our pains: it is His megaphone to rouse a deaf world."[3] God says that He is close to the brokenhearted and saves those who have been crushed in spirit (Ps. 34:18). He is the Father of mercies and the God of all comfort (2 Cor. 1:3). Jesus was portrayed as a man of sorrows and well acquainted with grief (Isa. 53:3). And Jesus was repeatedly referred to as a friend of sinners (Matt. 11:19; Luke 7:34). The Lord knows exactly how to minister to those who are in the midst of affliction, and our family watched God care for Walker and Laney after they lost Oakleigh.

There's a parable Jesus tells in the Gospel of Mark about the kingdom of God being likened to seed growing. Jesus says,

> "The kingdom of God is as if a man should scatter seed on the ground. He sleeps and rises night and day, and the seed sprouts and grows; he knows not how. The earth produces by itself, first the blade, then the ear, then the full grain in the ear. But when the grain is ripe, at once he puts in the sickle, because the harvest has come." (4:26–29)

I love this portrayal of God's work in people's lives because it's so clear that God is ultimately the One who makes things grow, including any spiritual life (cf. 1 Cor. 3:6). By this time in my friendship with Walker, we had talked so much about life, exchanged so many stories, and had walked through so much together that I felt like I knew him so well and knew how to pray for him as he was traveling out on the road. Yet, I was honestly amazed myself when it became clear that God was producing spiritual life in my friend. Our conversations over the phone began to drift Godward at *Walker's* initiative as he would tell me what different people shared with him about the song "Craig" or about his daughter Oakleigh as he was out on the road. Our text messages changed tone, as well, as Walker shared what he was reading.

* * *

It was a cool night in August when Walker and Laney met me and Laura at one of our favorite sushi restaurants in Franklin. Miso is a tiny restaurant off of Hillsboro Road, close to where Laura and I lived for several years. Our families had met there often, but this time it was just the four of us, a rare moment to connect without our ten kids between us. The Hayeses had prefaced the night by saying that Walker had something he wanted to share with us, but we didn't know exactly what to expect.

We caught up on how things were going on his tour and with the family. We ordered our sushi rolls, ready to enjoy every bite. That's when Walker started talking about Rosaria Butterfield's book, and how Laney had recommended it to him after the Bible study. He shared about the effect the book had on him, how he saw himself in Rosaria's story, and how much he appreciated how our family had loved on him the way Ken Smith and his wife had loved on Rosaria. He told us how he had bought a Bible and was reading through the gospels. And then he looked at me with a softness I had never seen in his eyes before, and he said, "Craig, I believe. I believe all of it."

I can't even describe this moment. I was more than a little stunned, but not surprised. To be honest, I was overwhelmed. I did not anticipate this conversation over sushi rolls. To make sure I was understanding my friend completely, I asked for clarification. I said, "Walk, are you telling me that you believe that Jesus is the Son of God, and that you want to live your life for His glory?" Walker responded gently with, "Yes, that's what I'm saying."

I immediately started crying and said, "Bro, I need to give you a hug." We stood up and I embraced Walker like I never had before—my brother. I tried to share with him how huge an answer to prayer this night was, and then I finally said through tears, "I'm gonna need a minute. I'm so sorry, but I'll be right back." I excused myself, headed straight to the men's restroom, locked the door, hit my knees, and in joyful, tearful worship, I gave thanks and praise to Jesus. Only God could do what had been done in Walker's life. He had transformed my friend from an alcoholic atheist who wanted nothing to do with Jesus to a worship-filled, believing follower of the Lord Jesus Christ. And He did it all right before my very eyes. What a privilege, what an honor, and what a sight to behold!

> God transformed my friend from an alcoholic atheist who wanted nothing to do with Jesus to a worship-filled, believing follower of the Lord Jesus Christ.

Once I gathered my composure, I sat back down, and Walker, Laney, Laura, and I had the most cheerful and heartfelt fellowship of our lives. We talked for hours, and when the restaurant closed, we took our conversation outside. We walked through an underground tunnel connecting the local shopping center to a neighborhood across the street. We talked about everything—our separate journeys to Nashville. The day we all met. The sister-dogs we shared.

The van we gave the Hayeses. The song, "Craig." Oakleigh, sweet little Oakleigh. The pain, the grief of her loss. The hope of heaven. Redeeming

Grace. The church, the gospel, the good news that Christ died for sinners—for us! The joy of Walker's salvation. It was an unforgettable evening, and we all knew then that *everything* had changed.

WALKER

About three months after I believed, and two years since we'd lost Oakleigh, Laney and the kids and I were at church. Laney stepped out of the service for a second during worship, and I noticed we had, for some odd reason, sat on the right side again. We were actually in the exact same row where we were on that dreadful baby dedication day. The band started jamming "It Is Well." I fell apart . . . in a good way . . . I just thought about Oakleigh and how the Lord had strategically given us that experience to engage us in a relationship with Him. How merciful that my daughter's life, though it was brief, had an eternal effect. I couldn't have sung if I'd tried because Jesus' love was squeezing the tears out of me. The song eventually ended, and Laney returned to her seat next to me. I whispered, "You missed 'It Is Well'!" She whispered back, "I just held a baby in the nursery, and it felt good." We stood there together speechless at the awesome power of God and His redeeming grace. It was well with our souls.

Since we lost Oakleigh, I've met several families who've also had a stillborn. It's a club you never wanted be a part of but you're so glad there's other people in it. I wrote this song for Oakleigh. It's about a father I met that impacted me deeply. I was struggling early on with how to respond to the "how many kids do y'all have?" question. I hated just saying "six" to avoid the awkwardness.

Oakleigh
Walker Hayes 2019

Hey Oakleigh, it's me, Dad, I miss you.
Just thought I'd stop by on my way home,
Catch the sunset with you.
Got asked how many kids we had again today
Still don't know what to say.

The truth makes it awkward
But just 'cause you're in heaven
doesn't mean you're not my daughter
So I said what I always say,
"Man, we just had our seventh, but we lost her."
But this guy was different
He didn't get weird
Or say things like, "Hey, least you still got six here."
He said, "Man, I'm so sorry, we lost a little girl, too."
And I felt like it was OK to feel like I do.

(Chorus)
Even though I know you're somewhere better
I don't want the world to forget you
Oakleigh, I will always say seven
Six on earth, and one in heaven.

His Oakleigh's name was Plum like the fruit, cute, right?
I had to know the reason
He said they named her that because when she was born they were in season
We talked about the hurt and the hope we shared
Wondered what you and Plum and Jesus were prob'ly up to up there
Maybe braiding each other's hair
We talked about loss and how fragile it taught you life was in a minute

How it's a club that you never wanna be a part of but you're so glad there's
other people in it

(Chorus)

So I guess that's all for today
I brought you some fresh flowers
And a plum
I guess for the ants to devour
I promise I will never keep you like a secret even though we couldn't keep you
Cuz you just never know who might have an Oakleigh too . . .

Meeting Jesus has changed me. That transformation that I begged Laney to prove actually happens is now happening in me. I'm not who I was. I am a new creation and getting newer every day. Ask my friends. Ask Craig! Now, one of my deepest desires is to see someone come to Jesus. To watch their heart soften and surrender it all to Him. To see their eyes widen with excitement and wonder as they begin to understand His love for them. I would like to see that over and over again.

CRAIG

GROWING UP PLAYING BASEBALL, I was one of those kids who played two positions: right field and the bench. I'm not the greatest athlete in the world anyway, so right field was probably the safest spot for me when our team was on the field. Every time someone got up to bat, I would pray for the batter to hit the ball in another direction. Things were even scarier when it was our team's turn to bat. Anyone who has played Little League baseball knows that batting can be a terrifying experience, even on a good day. You're up there all alone, with every eye in the bleachers and on the field focused on you. That's great if you're a star athlete and thrive off of the attention of a solid hit, but it's not so great if you're a mediocre athlete, like me, batting at the end of the line, and you just don't want to let your team down.

After I struck out for the twenty-third time in a row (I know it was twenty-three times because all my teammates in the dugout were counting) my coach called me over to the pitcher's mound where he was standing, looked me square in the eye and sympathetically said, "You're having a hard time, aren't you, Coop?" I just nodded with my head hung low. Then, it was as if a light bulb went off in Coach Scott's head. He turned us both around, faced the outfield, and said, "Craig, do me a favor and read me that sign in center field." I looked up at my coach, then looked as hard as I could in the direction he was pointing and finally said, "Coach, you know nobody can see past second base from here." He turned and yelled for my parents seated in the bleachers and said, "Your boy needs glasses!"

That week, my parents took me to the eye doctor who confirmed my coach's suspicions, and it wasn't long before I was wearing my first pair of glasses. Somehow, the doctor also convinced my parents that I needed sport goggles for baseball. Looking completely ridiculous but feeling as if a whole new world had opened up to me ("Look, I can see the *leaves* on those trees!"), our family set off to the next baseball game with me sporting a brand-new pair of huge, tinted goggles.

I didn't have much time to prepare or practice before it was my turn to bat. I could see the sweat dangling off the pitcher's nose. I could clearly make out the numbers on everyone's dusty jerseys. I could understand the facial expressions of the parents in the stands. I could read the sign in center field. But most importantly, I could see the ball in the pitcher's hand.

The first pitch came . . . and I completely freaked out. I jumped away from the plate, dropped the bat on the ground, and screamed for dear life. It was the first time I had seen the ball!

At this point, I was shaking, but managed to pick the bat back up. Dusting the dirt off, I stood with my right knee trembling, waiting for the second pitch. It felt like everything was happening in slow motion when the ball was released, floating its way through the humid air, and for the first time in twenty-four at-bats, I connected with the ball in a loud *crack*!

The sound to my ears was as new as the sight to my eyes, as I watched the ball climb through the windows of my tinted sport goggles up, up, and up, over the heads of the infielders, over the heads of the outfielders, and finally all the way over the head of the scoreboard. I had broken my slump with a homerun! Arms lifted in the air, I bounced my way victoriously past first, second, and third base before jumping on home plate like I had just landed on the moon. I was awarded the game ball that day and can still hear my mom exclaiming, "That's my child!"

It's amazing what proper vision can do for us. It literally changes everything.

There's a story in the Gospel of John about Jesus healing a man who was blind from birth. People asked Jesus why the man was born blind; did he sin, or did his parents sin? Jesus said it wasn't because of the sins of either him or his parents that he was born blind, but that the work of God might be displayed in him. Then Jesus spit on the ground, made mud with His saliva, put it on the man's eyes, and told him to wash in the pool of Siloam. The man did as Jesus instructed, and once he had washed, he could *see*. For the first time, this man had sight.

> **It's amazing what proper vision can do for us. It literally changes everything.**

Instead of being excited about the blind man receiving sight, some of the religious people were ticked off. They had created all sorts of rules of what a person could and couldn't do, and because Jesus had made mud with His saliva and put it on the man's eyes on the Sabbath, they saw Jesus as a rule breaker. A man who had been born blind encountered Jesus, experienced a miracle and received sight, and the religious people criticized Jesus for healing on the Sabbath.

Jesus ironically said that He came into the world that those who do not see may see, and those who see may become blind. What does this mean? Those who eventually recognize their spiritual darkness can receive the light of life that Jesus brings, but those who think they can already see will be blinded by their own pride. The Pharisees of Jesus' time thought they already had perfect vision, but they couldn't recognize the Savior when He was standing right in front of them. The blind man, on the other hand, received sight and actually *saw* the Savior (John 9).

The Bible talks a lot about our ability to see. It speaks not just about physical eyesight, but the eyes of our hearts.

If we think we have perfect vision, we'll never go to the eye doctor to get our eyes checked. And if we fancy ourselves as having flawless spiritual insight, we might not even recognize the real Jesus when He appears on the scene of our lives. But the good news for people with weak vision is that Jesus came to bring recovery of sight to those who need it. There's a prayer the Apostle Paul records in the book of Ephesians, asking that the eyes of our hearts would be enlightened, that they would be opened to the hope we have in Jesus (Eph. 1:18). When Jesus stoops to open our eyes, the rest of the world starts making a lot more sense.

I personally want to see people's eyes opened to the glory of Jesus. I want *everyone* to feel the joy of the Lord singing over them. To know that God delights in you, and that your life matters to God and the world around you. To know that you don't have to be the most gifted person in the world to make a difference. You don't have to be the most gregarious at parties. You don't have to be the smartest person in the room. You don't have to have an influential platform or massive presence on social media. If you just entrust yourself to God and live a faithful life of loving others, God can do amazing things through you. It may even surprise you how He is able to use you! But one thing's for sure: God is watching over you, and the day is coming when you will be rewarded for even the smallest acts of kindness you do in His name. If it doesn't happen in this life, it will most certainly happen in the next. Jesus said whoever gives a little one even a cup of cold water in His name will not lose his reward (Matt. 10:42). That's why, with affectionate desire for the eternal good and happiness of others, we should be ready to share not only the gospel of God, but also all that we are and all that we have with the dear people God has put in our paths (1 Thess. 2:8). We want to see them see His goodness.

In my opinion, there is nothing on this earth as glorious as the eyes of a new believer. I've watched stunning sunsets and sunrises. I've seen snow-capped mountains that have taken my very breath away. I've stood on the precipice of the Grand Canyon in all its glory amid the hushed "Wows" of amazed onlookers, and I have listened to the mighty rushing waters of Niagara Falls and have felt its mist on my skin. I've been immersed in a total solar eclipse and have felt the tingling of every hair on my skin as the moon has completely covered the sun with a midday darkness causing every creature in its vicinity to respond in awe. I've even had the joy of experiencing the sights, sounds, and wonders of an African safari while on a ministry trip to Rwanda. As one of my favorite songwriters, Rich Mullins, has sung: "There is so much beauty around us for just two eyes to see, but everywhere I go, I'm looking."[4] I love to celebrate all of God's good gifts, and I'm on a search for all the beauty around us in this broken world. Yet, there is no sight that for me has rivaled the magnificence of seeing the look inside the eyes of a new believer. It's a wonder of all wonders, a miracle of all miracles. It points to life eternal in the new heavens and new earth. I want to see that look over and over and over again. That's the look I saw in Walker's eyes when we sat at Miso and he shared his newly discovered joy in Jesus.

The work of God is displayed every single time someone is given spiritual sight; it's a new creation. Perhaps Jesus is opening your eyes for the first time as you read our story. I would give anything I own to see that look in your eyes!

10

A
PATH

WALKER

A little over a year ago, Laney and I were house shopping. We had the kids out with us and were hopping from neighborhood to neighborhood dreaming out loud. We had been in the same house for about fifteen years and were honestly pretty settled. Still, we enjoyed playing "what-if" from time to time, looking around at what was available. We found this brand-new home we loved; it was right outside of Nashville, and we called Craig and Laura to swing by and check it out with us. They met us there and we all oohed and aahed at the house. They loved it too! While we were looking at the new construction, Laura mentioned that her neighbor was about to put their house on the market. We had been to the Coopers' house a zillion times but never really noticed what the house next door looked like. Laura called her neighbor and asked if we could have a little impromptu showing. We felt bad swinging by while they were in the house and before they'd even had a chance to put a "for sale" sign up.

The family was super sweet to let us drop in. It was a couple with three kids and a dog and a cat or two. And they were all just hanging around while we looked through the house. It was actually pretty nice to tour it fully furnished and while life was happening. I could easily imagine our crew living there. So much so that I literally took a look at the family room, walked back outside, and called our financial advisor! I just knew. Laney and the kids continued to look around inside and upstairs while I figured out how to make an offer on a house. It had been a while since I'd done that.

I can't tell you how weird this act of spontaneity was for me. I mean, I have always been impulsive and spontaneous and historically have made many large decisions on complete whims, but me choosing to live close to someone was not what I did. Maybe Jesus was turning this island into something else.

And the Coopers actually wanted us to live next door! That blows my mind. I'm telling you, we look cute on the 'Gram but in person, we're a lot. However, the Coopers didn't bat one eye at the inevitable problems that come with real community. They actually invited us.

The week we moved in, the country shut down because of COVID. It was nothing short of miraculous how smoothly the move went and how much we would need each other during the year-long lockdown. We quarantined together. I have no idea what the Hayes kids and the Cooper kids would have done without each other. I have no idea what I would have done without Craig and what Laney would have done without Laura. Our kids started a band, Craig and I wrote songs, and Laura and Laney did puzzles. I found out I'm pretty awesome at dominoes.

One of the first nights we were there, we all stood in our backyards embracing the wonderful fact that we could step outside and see each other. Craig and I were talking on my back porch and decided the fence needed to come down.

We tried our best to take a section of the fence out the right way, then gave up and just ripped it out. And that's exactly what happened in our friendship. The walls had come down. Two complete strangers were neighbors, were family. Nothing between us, just Christ, bringing us toward community and toward Himself.

This path, the fence coming down, being neighbors with best friends could not be further from my human nature or my personality. I think I'm a four on the Enneagram. An Individualist who tends to struggle with intimate community. I move away from the herd, not next door.

One of the coolest things that has happened since we've lived here is this book. While the country was shut down, Craig wrote and wrote and wrote and wrote. Craig writes all of his sermons out, and it is beyond obvious that God has given him a gift and a desire to write. Now, I love all things that involve dreaming. So, if anyone expresses even the slightest interest in chasing one, I love to encourage them. Especially Craig. Craig writes like he preaches. When you read what he writes, you can tell he fiercely believes what he is saying. As a believer, it's like you get to re-hear the good news for the first time. As an unbeliever, even when I wasn't buying the good news, I found myself wanting it to be true. That sentence makes me laugh now because the gospel is free. God isn't selling anything; He's just giving us Jesus.

It's just crazy—the overwhelming redeeming grace of Jesus. To taste it. To watch its ripple effect. It is rare that Craig and I see each other and don't dwell on the mystery of Jesus. That two guys would collide in this world and become brothers in Christ. That our families would be more than family. That the glory of God and the mercy of Jesus would be revealed in a worn-out path between two houses in middle Tennessee. I don't understand it, but I want to share it. I want to be a friend like Craig was and is to me.

The Coopers are not our saviors, but they know the man who is. Their relationship with Jesus had an eternal impact on a very-messed-up family, and the walls that I used to imagine covered with platinum records are now covered with handwritten Scripture. The platinum record is in the garage somewhere behind the bikes. A section of fence that once divided two households is also in the garage. Man, is it nice to know someone and be really known! When we hang with the Coopers, not one ounce of me is trying. We can just be. I truly believe that's how Jesus wants us. Just us. Mess included. He wants us in our Sunday worst, and that's what we wear to the Coopers' house.

CRAIG

IT TOOK ME AND WALKER about half an hour to rip out a section of the fence that separated our two backyards. It was one of the first things we did together after his family moved into the house next door.

We were sitting on the back porch of the Hayeses' new home drinking coffee and talking about how incredible it was that after years of friendship, we were now brothers in Christ and next-door neighbors. Walker looked left toward my home and said, "Let's surprise the girls and take out a section of that fence." My eyes lit up, and we both jumped to our feet and ran immediately to the fence to do the deed. Over the years, our wives, Laura and Laney, have jokingly called us dreamers. In that moment, we were both doers. As the fence link was enthusiastically removed and stored away, the path connecting our homes officially formed.

Walker and I have talked a lot about that fence. The spot is both literal and symbolic for us. We can review the details of our lives and see how the gospel—the good news that brings believers into a relationship with God—has broken down barriers for us and has brought us together like the ripping out of the fence between our homes. This path is one of personal failures and the faithfulness of God. It's a path of rejection and redemption. It's a path of loss and love. And it's a path well-worn with pain uniting us to each other and to God.

The truth is, there's a path we all share. The fundamental commonalities that mark us as humans are much greater than our differences. They are universal, and the remedy is the same: we are all in need of a Savior.

Jesus said, "I am the way, and the truth, and the life" (John 14:6). Jesus *is* the Savior, the path to true and lasting meaning in this life and the next. He is the way.

When I step out of our back deck and see how the grass has been worn by the daily pitter-pattering of fourteen pairs of feet (and our collective dogs), I just look down at that path and smile. I think of Jesus, who He is and what He has done for us, and I rejoice that the gospel He brings breaks down barriers that separate us from God and each other. Jesus welcomes us to His table, just as we are, and the hospitality we enjoy there with Him breaks down walls and tears out fences.

> **The fundamental commonalities that mark us as humans are much greater than our differences. They are universal, and the remedy is the same: we are all in need of God.**

One of the most thoughtful and creative gifts Laura and I have ever received is a wooden plank that hangs in our kitchen as a decorative frame for photos. We currently have pictures of each of our four kids clipped on it. To the casual observer, it just looks like a beautifully painted board—a rustic light-green tint with four white sections jutting from the frame, each with a clip for a photo. But to us, it is packed with significance.

Back in Knoxville, we had opened our home to our friends, a family of six, to live with us for about six months after our friend Rebecca discovered she had environmentally related health issues in their own home. We had a hunch that she was getting sick because of something in their house, but no one could put their finger on the cause of her illness. We had encouraged their family to stay in our home while we traveled to visit Laura's family for a short trip over the summer, and when they stayed there, Rebecca was healthy. When she returned home, she got sick again. So, we said, "Just move in with us." Our daughter, Penelope, was a baby at the time. They had four kids, and we had four kids, so the twelve of us lived together in our four-bedroom home (just before our family moved to Nashville). In many ways, I believe God used this time together to prepare us for our friendship with the Hayeses, as He certainly gave us a taste of the joy of immersive community.

> *Jesus welcomes us to His table, just as we are, and the hospitality we enjoy there with Him breaks down walls and tears out fences.*

The wooden plank that hangs as a picture frame in our kitchen was a gift from our friend Rebecca, long after their family lived with us. On the back of the picture frame are the words of a Celtic poem, pronouncing blessings over our home:

> *May these walls be filled with laughter,*
> *May it reach from floor to rafter,*
> *May the roof keep out the rain,*
> *May the sunshine warm each window pane,*
> *And may the door be open wide*
> *To let the Good Lord's love inside.*
> *May love and laughter light your days*
> *And warm your heart and home.*
> *May good and faithful friends be yours,*
> *Wherever you may roam.*

May peace and plenty bless your world
With joy that long endures
May all life's passing seasons
Bring the best to you and yours.[1]

I believe the Lord has honored this blessing. The walls of our home have been beat up a bit through normal wear and tear, and Laura says it's long past time to paint, but our home has been filled with laughter and joy from the floors to the rafters. Our doors have been open wide, and God has smiled on us with good and faithful friends. Having the Hayeses next door has been one of the greatest blessings we've ever received.

Below this Celtic blessing, our friend Rebecca wrote the following about the decorative plank she gave as a gift: "This was a baseboard in our house that came out during the remodel. Now you have a piece of our house in yours. Thank you for your hospitality and kindness, dear friends."

When you give a piece of your heart and home to others, you may soon find a piece of their heart and home beautifully decorating yours.

Through the pages of this book, Walker and I have sought to bring a piece of our home into yours.

We pray that you, too, would experience the joy of Jesus, the joy of your own torn-down fences, the joy of your own path of connection and community.

Our prayer for each and every person who reads this book is that you would experience the love of Jesus as we have, and that the doors to your home would be open wide "to let the Good Lord's love inside."

We pray that you, too, would experience the joy of Jesus, the joy of your own torn-down fences, the joy of your own path of connection and community.

We hope this book has encouraged you to live life to the fullest, love others sacrificially, and let the light of Christ shine in you and through you. Jesus loves you. Your life matters, and we're so glad you're here!

WALKER

Last year, Laney and I tried to foster children. Unfortunately, we were ineligible for the process because our house is considered "full." One of the most difficult things to grieve since losing Oakleigh has been the loss of having more children all together. It would be unsafe for Laney to get pregnant. She was devastated that we were done. It was just hard for us, circumstances telling us we weren't able to have any more kids. Don't get me wrong, we are beyond grateful for the children we have; we just didn't have any intentions of stopping there. Now, I know this is crazy. I know most people are reading this thinking, "What, six isn't enough?" I completely understand that assessment. However, we just didn't feel done. We didn't even know what that meant but we both talked and prayed about it continually.

When fostering fell through, we prayed that God would open a door for us to adopt. We actually prayed that the Lord would lead an expecting mother to our porch. We considered the traditional adoption route but it just felt greedy given the fact we had a basketball team and one on the bench already. We even prayed that the Lord would release us from those desires. That we would wake up and feel finished and just look forward to the future possibility of grandkids. Over time, neither happened.

Then, a couple months later, we heard that Lela's old gymnastics coach had just had his first child. Laney texted them to say congrats and "Holla if y'all ever need a babysitter." Thinking to herself, "There ain't no way first-time parents are dropping their newborn off at the house with six kids." Lo and behold, Marco and Adrienne texted Laney back and asked if she was serious about the babysitting offer. Adrienne said they were about to get back to work and actually needed childcare. Laney and I were dumbfounded. So was our entire family.

The first time Adrienne brought her over to the house, we had to taper our excitement to a non-creepy level. We were all just standing at the door when it opened. A little too jacked to meet this little one. The wildest thing about this whole story is that this little girl we take care of, this precious little blessing that absolutely lights our house up five days a week, is named Oakley. Sure, the spelling is different, but come on. Tell me that ain't God.

Lord, You had my salvation in Your pocket all along. You knew Craig before the world was created. You know Oakleigh and Oakley. Lord, I pray for things, and You already know the face I'm going to make when the answers are more redemptive than my brain could have ever imagined. God, I just ask that somehow You use these stories, Craig's and my friendship, Laney and Laura's friendship, and our children's account of what they have witnessed to further Your kingdom. Just like You did with the song, "Craig." Just like You did with the love of Christ through Craig and his family. Father, thank You for the minivans and many ways You drive us to Your Son, Jesus Christ.

AFTERWARD

CRAIG

SEVERAL YEARS AGO, I attended an end-of-the-year awards ceremony at my daughter Charlotte's elementary school. Her teacher had carefully and creatively planned an award for each child, individually represented by a particular candy bar or treat. With about twenty-six kids in the class, this was no small feat, and I was impressed with the whole idea.

Charlotte's teacher started by honoring the boys with rewards before transitioning to certificates, candy, and acclaim for each girl. As any parent can imagine, throughout the event I was eagerly anticipating Charlotte's award and wondering how her teacher would communicate about my daughter. I thought she couldn't go wrong with any candy when describing Charlotte because of how sweet she is (she's our most tender child).

Because I wasn't sure when Charlotte's turn would be, I took a separate video of every girl's award. I watched as "The Starburst Award" was given to one child for being a star academically. I witnessed the "Gummy Bear Award" which identified the most huggable student in the second-grade class. (Apparently, she greeted the teacher with a big hug every morning and multiple times throughout the day!) One of Charlotte's closest friends, Kinley, received the "Three Musketeers Award" for always being sweet and working well with others in the class. Charlotte's other friend CeCe received the "Kit Kat Award" for sharing fun ideas throughout the year with her cheerful chit-chat, and I personally got a kick out of the "Milky Way Award" for the girl with the out-of-this-world ideas.

After watching countless honors doled out, Charlotte's teacher announced that she had two certificates left in her hand, and I thought she must have saved the best for last. But then she shared that two students together would be receiving the "Rolo Award" for continually rolling into class with perfect attendance. Since the first week of January that year, the Cooper family had at least one child sick among our crew nearly every week, so if there was one award I knew that none of my kids would receive that year, it was perfect attendance. After the Rolo Awards were distributed, the teacher's hands were empty.

No more candy. No more chocolate. No more honors. No more kind words. No more certificates. No more awards.

Right there with her dad and family in attendance, my sweet Charlotte had been completely forgotten.

Now, I'm a firm believer in the providence of God, so I sat there quietly wondering about it all. I wasn't upset. I was just contemplative. Of every child in the classroom, I knew the Lord chose Charlotte for this moment. And, let's be honest, these are not moments you easily forget. I've forgotten so much about my childhood, but I can still remember my second-grade teacher, Mrs. Brown (mainly because she waved a strange wand over our heads during tests, repeating the phrase, "Wammy Jammy," "Wammy Jammy," "Wammy Jammy,"—yep, you can't make this stuff up).

I knew Charlotte would remember this moment, so I began quietly praying for the Lord to minister to her as only He can. Right then, Charlotte's friend CeCe said, "Charlotte, where's your award?" My daughter quietly replied, "I don't know." Then CeCe stood up and interrupted the teacher who had moved on to introducing the

End-of-the-Year Slideshow, and she said, "Miss V, Charlotte didn't get an award."

It was clear no award or certificate had been prepared, but somehow her teacher quickly rummaged through desk drawers and found a big bag of Twizzlers for my girl. She announced to the entire class that she had somehow accidentally lost Charlotte's certificate but that she was receiving the Twizzler Award. I leaned down to Charlotte, gave her a huge hug and said, "You know, sweetheart, Twizzlers are awesome. Those are Daddy's favorite." With that, my sweet Charlotte handed me the whole bag and say, "You can have them, Daddy." What's amazing is she was smiling when she said it. I said, "No way, baby girl; those are all yours."

I was so proud of the way she responded. There were no tears, no evident sign of sadness; no sense that anything was wrong; just tender, accepting joy. I know it's good for my kids to experience moments like this, because this stuff happens.

I know it will happen again to Charlotte, because it's happened to all of us. And it stinks when it does. I wanted so badly to lean down to Charlotte, right there in front of the whole class and encourage her to take it all in. I wanted to say, "Sweetheart, you're going to be overlooked at times, but you will never be forgotten by God."

What's funny to me is that Charlotte didn't appear to even need the encouragement. She had already moved on, laughing during the end-of-the-year slide show. But I needed to be reminded of God's Word. I thought of that passage in Isaiah 49: "Can a woman forget her nursing child, that she should have no compassion on the son of her womb? Even these may forget, yet *I will not forget you.* Behold, I have engraved you on the palms of my hands; your walls are continually before me" (vv. 15–16).

I thought of how Jesus said, "Are not five sparrows sold for two pennies? And not one of them is forgotten before God. Why, even the hairs of your head are all numbered. Fear not; you are of more value than many sparrows" (Luke 12:6–7).

I thought of how Charlotte's friend, CeCe, obviously didn't forget her. She literally stood up for her. I thought of how that act from CeCe must please the Lord and how people need someone to stand up for them at times and say, "Don't forget this one!" I thought of what a good friend CeCe was and how I want to be that kind of friend to others.

And then I thought of how Walker has been that kind of friend to me. Walker's been my CeCe. In my lowest moments, he's been right there by my side, encouraging and strengthening me (and he was doing that even before he was a believer!). What a good friend!

After the Hayeses moved next door, I found myself nursing a failing start-up staffing firm in the midst of the pandemic, and I was struggling with significant anxiety and even depression. Through it all, Walker was a constant encouragement to me. One night during dinner together, as I was apologizing to the Hayeses for feeling so low and burdened, Walker just looked at me with compassion and said, "It's okay, bro . . . We love you low." What an expression of gospel grace and care! We. Love. You. Low. Isn't that what Jesus does for us? He loves us in our lowest state (Rom. 5:8).

On another occasion, Walker and I were sitting on his front porch, and I was sharing some significant challenges with him, and he asked to pray for me on the spot. "God, I pray for my friend like I've never prayed for him before, please help him." Walker essentially picked me up and carried me right into the presence of God. I was so strengthened by his genuine prayers and care. You can't do community this close and be all sunshine and rainbows. The Hayeses have seen the worst in us, and yet they still love us. All of this speaks to me of the love of the Savior. It's an unconditional kind of love.

It's also a generous love. Y'all, we came home from a family trip one day to find that our broken dishwasher had been completely replaced with a brand-new state-of-the-art appliance that Walker and Laney had bought for us and Walker installed himself while we were away. We thought we were coming home to a big problem to fix; instead, we came home to a big problem solved. We've shared life completely in its joys and trials, and I thank God for the friendship we have with the Hayeses, as it truly is a gift.

My prayer for all who read this book is that somehow the pages here would breathe hope into the very depths of your soul, that you can have a friend in Jesus and experience the kind of friendship with others that breaks down walls and offers hope in the midst of the hurts of this life. God is real. He is good. He does, in fact, hear our prayers. He does, in fact, care very deeply about you and your circumstances. He knows all the intricate details of your life and nothing in it is trivial or mundane when God is with you.

This book is so ironic to me because I've long desired to be an author, but I was so hesitant to speak or write about any of *this*. Honestly, our friendship with the Hayeses has been so precious that I've guarded it from the public eye. It took Walker's encouragement and the realization that just as the song "Craig" was his personal thank-you note to our family, so this book could be a collective thank-you note to Jesus Himself.

Now, that's something I could get onboard with.

So, here it is—the street-level stuff of our daily lives offered as a thank-you to Jesus Himself. Lord, this book is all for You. Please use our stories and all that You've done in our lives for the advancement of the gospel of Your grace and the glory of Your great name. And may our lives and the friendship You've formed between the Coopers and the Hayeses be like a signpost pointing all who see it directly to You.

WALKER

We still live next door to Craig, and I don't plan on moving anytime soon. Craig and I regularly ponder our story. How it began, how it unfolded, and how it's still being written by Jesus, the author and finisher of our faith. I couldn't even write a song expressing how grateful I am for my testimony . . . to have had this opportunity to pour it out in a book. Seriously, y'all, ask Craig. I always encouraged him to write a book. I had no idea we would write it together. And to be 100% honest, like the song, I don't think Craig or I really wrote it at all . . . the Lord did. We just get to share it. With words, no one can do Jesus justice. He's all I wanna sing about. He's all I wanna talk about. He's all I wanna live about.

I'm back on the road. As we were coming out of the COVID shutdown, I released a song called "Fancy Like," and it's been lingering at number one on The Hot 100 country for months. I've finally written something you've heard! Funny to me that I spent the first two years as a believer writing dozens of songs about Jesus, but they never really moved the needle. And then I write one about "Applebee's on a date night" and the whole world is doing the dance. Oh Lord, You and Your mysterious ways. "Fancy Like" is by far my biggest hit, but "Craig" is my favorite song to sing every night. I'm always nervous as I begin telling my testimony. I know there are those in the audience who are just like I was before I met Jesus, thinking, "If I'd a wanted to go to church, I'd a just gone to church." I speak to them specifically when I introduce the song and explain how well I can relate, but I can't not share the love of Christ. The same love that met me through Craig. I guess you could say I take the bar to church for a few minutes.

I actually just finished re-recording the song "Craig," featuring the band MercyMe. I am thrilled with how it turned out and can't wait for the world to hear it. By the time this book comes out, I hope you will know it by heart.

This chapter, this book, doesn't end like a cliché Christian movie where we win the championship, Laney gets pregnant, and we live happily ever after. I'm still a sinner. I still want to drink sometimes. I still wish we could have another baby. I still miss Oakleigh and wonder if I'm even allowed to technically say "I miss her" since we never really met. I love and hate my job, depending on the day and what time it is. Even though Laney and I have Jesus in common, we still manage to find things to fight about. I'm so grateful for what "Fancy Like" has done for my career, but I'm struggling to find balance between work and family. I also check myself often, fearing that I've made fame and recognition my god. That work is my new beer. But praise God, while I am not perfect, my Savior is, and my need for Him only grows.

I have different dreams now. I have rest even when I'm tired. I have hope, and His name is Jesus. I want Him. I want my kids to know Him. I wanna do whatever it is I'm supposed to do on this earth and then peace out and meet Jesus. I can't wait to hear Him say, "Glad you're here."

ACKNOWLEDGMENTS

CRAIG

OH, MY—THERE ARE SO MANY people to thank.

First of all, *Glad You're Here* would not exist apart from the work of our acquisitions editor, Trillia Newbell. Trillia, we truly can't thank you enough for believing in this project, for championing it among the Moody Publishers team, and for your consistent and specific encouragement throughout the twists and turns of the development of this book to deliver it to the world in its present form. For any good that God does in the world through *Glad You're Here*, we will forever be grateful for you!

To Mackenzie Conway, our development editor: It is no small task to work with two first-time authors who have very distinct voices, blending separate perspectives together to formulate such a cohesive work. That effort of constant collaboration is painstaking work, and we thank God for you and how you helped us bring this all together. *Glad You're Here* is a much better book than it was before it landed in your hands. Thank you also to Randall Payleitner, Connor Sterchi, Ryan June, Erik Peterson, Ashley Torres, Melissa Zaldivar, and the entire team at Moody Publishers for taking on this project. It's our prayer that this book would be a blessing to Moody and to many for years to come!

Thank you to Mark Freeman and Provisions Group for hiring a full-time pastor to be a full-time recruiter back in the fall of 2012, opening the door for me to work in the recruiting world while also helping plant a church. Mark, your generosity has inspired me for years, and it was such an honor to work with you and for you. You watched this book unfold, and I want you to know I've never forgotten that God used you to make the way for it.

I want to personally thank the pastors and members of Redeeming Grace Church for your example. Dave, Howard, Jason, and Jon, it's been one of the greatest privileges of my life to partner together with you in pastoral ministry. Thank you for friendship, prayers, and constant support. RGC, we hope you're encouraged as you read this book because it truly is a fruit of your ministry.

Thank you to Kris Kelso, John Duval, Jeremy Krulikowski, Connor Shank, Brian Clarke, and Steve Hoppe for your help, counsel, and encouragement during some of the toughest times I've walked through, and thank you to Jonathan Oldacre and Holly Robinson for your expertise and support when I needed it most.

Dave and Krista Sagraves, David and Emilee Stanley, Bryan and Shi Morris, Fred and Christina Wiechmann: This book is all about friendship and you all are faithful friends. I look forward to every second we are able to spend together and laugh together. Being with you all gives me a glimpse of the pleasures of heaven and makes me long for the day when our capacity for joy in Christ is without limit!

Dad, you are the greatest man I have ever known. You have modeled steadfast, sacrificial love, hard work, cheerfulness, and generosity. You've been such an amazing father, and my respect for you could not be any greater. I love you and I hope this book encourages you as a fruit of your labor in my life. Mom, your generosity over the years has been over the top—I have no doubt God used your example to inspire me as we gave a van to the Hayeses in a time of need. I love you. Tyson and Niki, Stu and Jenny, I've been so blessed having you as my brothers and sisters-in-law. Stu, thanks for letting me use the "mafia story" in this book—I love hearing you tell it! Mary Pat and Dick, Derek and Katie, John and Raleigh, thank you for welcoming me into the family and for decades of love and support.

Laura, my Love—thank you for embarking on this crazy adventure together. We've been through it all, haven't we? No one knows me better, and yet you still love me, and that speaks to me of the love of our Savior. The best earthly decision I've made in my life is asking you to marry me, and I'm so grateful you said "Yes." Thanks for being patient throughout this book writing process; you truly are an amazing woman. Karis, Joshua, Charlotte, and Penelope, you've brought us so much joy, and it's such an honor to be your Daddy. I love you!

Walker and Laney . . . wow. Thank you for being unflappable friends. Thank you for wanting to move next door (and for actually doing it!). That still blows me away. Thanks for being real with us and for being a safe place for us to be real with you. God smiled on the Cooper family when He brought you into our lives. Now y'all are family, and I can't believe we got to write this book together to tell our story to the world for the glory of Jesus.

Jesus, you're the One—You know this is all for You.

WALKER

Lord, I'm overwhelmed with gratitude. Thank you for Craig. Thank You for his family and their willingness to do life with us. I love the beautiful part they play in my testimony. I couldn't work on this book without crying as I reflected on Your relentless pursuit of my heart. Jesus, please embrace people with these words.

Craig. Dude. Somebody's gonna buy a Bible after they read this.

Man, I love you. I have loved collaborating on this with you but I'm ready to read the next twenty books you write without me. I can only imagine how much the Lord loves using you. I hope my mansion is next to yours in heaven.

Appendix A
SONGS

"Lela's Stars"
Walker Hayes/Matt Jenkins/Tyrus Morgan

It's 3:42 a.m., eyes blood shot
Yawning in my Honda in a Costco parking lot
Waiting on the door to unlock so I can clock in early
And stock the cooler 'til I swear I need back surgery
Wondering what the hell I'm doing with my life
Wishing I was still in bed with my wife
Scribbling lyrics on the side of a styrofoam cup
Do my kids need their dad to grow up
Or keep chasing the dream
It ain't making no sense, no dollars
Am I a failure, or a father?
Father, help, look at the felt on my effed up ceiling
Had to bum thumbtacks from my nine-and-a-half-year-old daughter Lela
Just to keep it from coming down
Kinda like my tears when I count

(Chorus)
Lela's stars
The sky ain't fallin', it's just the roof of my car
Lela's stars
The sky ain't fallin', it's just the roof of my car
It's just the roof of my car

Man, I wish this coffee had a little Maker's in it
Eleven bucks an hour . . . that's less than twenty cents a minute
But, hey, it's a gig, and it's food in the refrigerator
It's time to get to work, but y'all, when I get off later
I'm gonna pick up this pen where I'm leaving off now
And get back to this song and show my children how to never give up
On something you love, something you want
Even when your check engine light is on
Nah, the future don't look bright but
It's like it's all going to be all right in the light of

(Chorus)

Pink and purple, green and blue, poor man's decorations
All I saw was a bunch of thumbtacks, she saw constellations
It's gonna be tough to get rid of this ride when the world gets my gift
'Cause I don't think they make new cars that come with

(Chorus)

It's just the roof of my car

"Beer In The Fridge"

Walker Hayes/Scot Sherrod/Shane McAnally/Matt Jenkins

I ran into your mom at church
She said I've been praying for you
Guess now that you've moved on
She ain't mad at me no more
The magnolias on old Shell Road smell so bittersweet
Sometimes I still wanna get messed up
But you'd be proud of me

(Chorus)
There's a beer in the fridge, last of 12
Sole survivor of my last all-nighter
In the back of the bottom shelf
It's gonna be there in the morning
Even though you won't
You're the reason I quit drinking
And the reason I wanna get drunk

I still look out for the cops when I'm driving around town
And I'm still not quite sure what to do with my hands in a crowd
There's a lot I can't remember and a lot I can't forget
One silver bullet in the chamber and I'm playing Russian Roulette

(Chorus)

I don't know why I keep it, I should probably pour it out
Guess I've got to live without you now
'Cause I couldn't live without

(Chorus)

"My Peace Has Been Purchased"
Walker Hayes/Craig Cooper 2020

God and I were enemies
Nothing but sin in me
Just another Adam eating apples
Off that forbidden tree
Dead man low-living,
Y'all I was so wicked
It's like my heart had a pulse
But my soul didn't
Y'all, I needed a remedy
Brand-new identity
But I was like a leper, who would ever
Be a friend of me
But God came close to me
Sent the One He loved the most to me
Jesus lived, and He died, and He rose for me

My peace has been purchased
My debts have been cleared
Held by God's purpose
My heart remains cheered
By the joy, of my salvation
I will not be shaken
I will worship
My peace has been purchased

I will not be anxious
All of my fears are vanquished
'Cause my Jesus took His blood
Down to the bank for us

We don't owe a thing
Death, where's your sting?
Hey, my victory's won,
I've been redeemed
by the King

Peace that surpasses
All comprehension
Laid down the price
For all my transgressions
On Calvary
Lord, You rescued me
Took my burdens
And gave rest to me
Bought me that
Peace that surpasses
All comprehension
Paid for in full
By your crucifixion
On Calvary
Lord, You bled for me
On the cross
In my stead for me

Jesus lived and He died, and He rose for me
My peace has been purchased

"The Broken"
Walker Hayes/Craig Cooper 2020

(Chorus)
I ain't nothing but a sinner, how am I sitting at this dinner
That the Savior's invited me to crash?
My Physician told the Pharisees He wasn't embarrassed to be
Associated with the outcasts
Just reclining with my Savior at the tax collectors' table
'Cause I'm chosen by the Chosen
That's some good news, am I right?
Thank God, the Bread of Life
Breaks bread with the broken

Two words, "follow me"
That's all Jesus said
I can only imagine the math
Matthew was doing in his head
When he heard that call and he rose
From that tax-collector booth
And left his love for empty riches
To go walking with the truth
He threw a feast honoring Jesus bringing rest to the restless
But the Scribes and Pharisees didn't approve of the guest list
Started grilling the disciples, Jesus spoke in their defense
Said, "I've not come to call the righteous but the sinners to repent"

(Chorus)

My Jesus, friend of strangers, lepers, lunatics and pricks,
Prostitutes, criminals, he didn't roll in no cliques
Said "It's not the well who need a Doctor but those who are sick"
I'd still be a drunk if Jesus didn't drink with alcoholics

Y'all, that's love how He suffered for the lost on the cross
How His blood is enough, we are new, we are washed
And when God looks at me, He sees the righteousness of Christ
And up in heaven's dining room, I'mma be sipping wine like

(Chorus)

That's some good news, am I right?
Thank God, the Bread of Life
Breaks bread with the broken
(Breaks bread with the broken)
That's some good news, am I right?
Thank God, the Bread of Life
Breaks bread with the broken
That's some good news, am I right?

"Now I Live for Christ Alone"
Walker Hayes/Craig Cooper 2020

Lead me not into temptation
Dwelling on the sins You saved me from
For in Christ I'm a new creation
The old has past, behold the new has come

I've been crucified with Christ
His nail-scarred hands outstretched for me
In Jesus' death now I have died
Gaining life eternally
I will glory in my Savior
His righteousness my very own
What grace, what love, what wonder!

Now I live for Christ alone
To the shame in my reflection
With my failures in your eyes
I will reject your rejection
All my Father sees is Christ

I will not set Your grace aside
Leaning on my fallen flesh
I accept the death that You died
Clothing me in righteousness

Appendix B
PICTURES

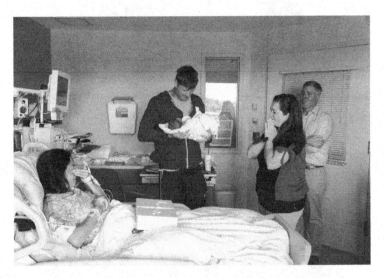

June 6, 2018. Oakleigh Klover Hayes. 7 pounds 13 ounces. 20 1/4 inches

Photo credit: Kalimana

Craig, Laura, Walker, and Laney celebrating the Hayeses buying the house next door.

Hayes and Cooper kids spending time together.

NOTES

Chapter 2: A Church

1. Charles Spurgeon, "The Best Donation" (No. 2234), April 5, 1891, sermon, Metropolitan Tabernacle, London, http://www.spurgeongems.org/sermon/chs2234.pdf.
2. Ray Ortlund, "New Members' Seminar," Immanuel Nashville, February 10, 2013.
3. Ray Ortlund, adapted from James Boyce, "Call to Worship," Immanuel Nashville.

Chapter 4: A Wednesday

1. Bob Goff (@bobgoff), Instagram photo, October 17, 2021, https://www.instagram.com/p/CVImHnuFAr-/.

Chapter 5: A Bar

1. Walker Hayes, "Daddy's Beer," boom., December 8, 2017.
2. "St. Patrick's Irish Hymn," in James Henthorn Todd, *St. Patrick Apostle of Ireland: A Memoir of His Life and Mission* (Dublin: Hodges, Smith, & Co., 1864), 428.
3. Gary Portnoy and Judy Hart Angelo, "Where Everybody Knows Your Name," *Music from Cheers*, August 13, 1982.

Chapter 6: A Van

1. Charles H. Spurgeon, *Beside Still Waters: Words of Comfort for the Soul* (Nashville: Thomas Nelson, 1999).

Chapter 7: A Song

1. Walker Hayes, "Craig," *boom.*, December 18, 2017.
2. Walker Hayes, *boom.*, Monument Records, a division of Sony Music Entertainment, December 18, 2017.
3. Dane Ortlund, *Gentle and Lowly: The Heart of Christ for Sinners and Sufferers* (Wheaton, IL: Crossway), 19–22.
4. Walker Hayes (@walkerhayes), "Have had some time at home these past few days and have done a lot of reflecting. This is something that's really been on my mind. Shot an email to my team but wanted to share with everyone . . ." Instagram photo, May 23, 2018, https://www.instagram.com/p/BjJAOpaHZKv/?taken-by=walkerhayes.

Chapter 9: A Friend

1. Horatio Spafford, "It Is Well with My Soul," composed by Philip Bliss, *Gospel Hymns No. 2*, Ira Sankey and Bliss, 1876.
2. Rosaria Butterfield, *The Secret Thoughts of an Unlikely Convert* (Pittsburgh, PA: Crown & Covenant Publications, 2014).
3. C. S. Lewis, *The Problem of Pain* (New York: HarperCollins Publishers, 1940), 90–91.
4. Rich Mullins, "Here in America," *A Liturgy, A Legacy, and a Ragamuffin Band*, 1993.

Chapter 10: A Path

1. Irish house blessing, author unknown.

WALKER HAYES is a Grammy–nominated singer/songwriter originally from Mobile, Alabama, signed to Monument Records. Throughout his career, he has released multi-Platinum singles "Fancy Like" and "You Broke Up With Me," performed on national television with *Good Morning America*, *Late Night with Seth Meyers*, *The Tonight Show Starring Jimmy Fallon*, and *The TODAY Show*, and been written about in the *LA Times*, *Esquire*, *Billboard*, and *Rolling Stone*.

A proud father of six, his music often centers around family, as is true with single "Craig"—a song about a neighbor who reached out to the Walker in a time of need. "Craig" was nominated for Song of the Year at the 2018 AIMP Nashville Awards and prompted Hayes to start the Be A Craig Fund to help other families in need. A new version of the track featuring MercyMe is on Hayes's album *Country Stuff the Album*. The song inspired this book.

To stay up to date with all things Walker Hayes, including new music, beacraig.org, socials, and more, scan QR code.

CRAIG COOPER is a gifted storyteller and Bible teacher. For over twenty years, he has spoken at numerous churches, men's retreats, college campuses, and various gatherings and has traveled across North America, South America, Europe, Africa, and India with a desire to see and serve the world. An encourager at heart, Craig's passion is to help people perceive the gifts of God in their lives and deploy them for Jesus' glory. Having served as one of the founding pastors of Redeeming Grace Church in Franklin, TN, Craig now resides in the greater Nashville area with his amazing wife, Laura, and their four kids as next-door neighbors to the Hayes family.

You can follow Craig on Instagram **@craigallencooper** and for more information or for speaking inquiries, please visit **craigallencooper.com**.